ILLUMINATING THE PERFORMANCE

ILLUMINATING THE PERFORMANCE

African and Arab Erotology

Habeeb Akande

RABAAH PUBLISHERS

First Published in England by Rabaah Publishers
7 Granary Square
Epping Place
London, N1 1FA
www.rabaah.com
admin@rabaah.com

Editor: Azeez Akande
Author: Habeeb Akande

Printed and bound by: CPI Group (UK) Ltd, Croydon, CR0 4YY

A catalogue record of this book is available from the British Library

ISBN-13: 978-0-9574845-3-5

Cover image:
Abdel Ghourm et Nour el Ain (French: Esclave d'Amour et Lumière des Yeux; English: Slave of Love and Light of my Eyes), 1900 by Étienne Nasreddine Dinet (d. 1929)

Dedicated to my father who taught me the principles of manliness.

TABLE OF CONTENTS

PREFACE

In the Name of Allah,[1] *the Most Beneficent, the Most Merciful. May He bless His Messenger, Muhammad the son of Abdullah.*

Praise be to God who has made a man's supreme delight in the private parts of a woman, and has made the male member the source of the greatest pleasure for women. Neither sex finds true satisfaction and great fulfilment until the man has penetrated the woman and they both reach mutual pleasure, simultaneously.

This book is a traditional guide on womanising and erotology (the art of sexual love and lovemaking) for the modern male, which I have named, *Illuminating the Performance: African and Arab Erotology.*[2] This book is based upon independent study of classic erotology texts, the views of African traditionalists and personal experience. This is *not* a book about mistreating, abusing, or taking advantage of vulnerable women. It *is* a book that is concerned with improving male confidence and sexual performance based upon traditional principles of manliness.

Behind the bravado that a lot of men display with women, lies a great deal of fear and insecurities. A lot of men rely on material items to attract and impress women due to a lack of self-confidence. Self-confidence

---

[1] Allah is the Arabic word for the One God.

[2] The title is in homage to the North African erotologist, Muhammad al-Nafzawi, author of *The Perfumed Garden of Sensual Delight*, who authored an erotological treatise of the name.

is one of the most attractive qualities women desire in men but it is not the only one. There are other qualities which men need to possess to satisfy a woman's emotional and physical desires which a lot of men are not aware about, erotologists have stated. Fortunately I was introduced to the subject of erotology a number of years ago and thought that it would be beneficial to write a book about this unknown topic from an African perspective.

African Perspective on Erotology and Womanising

In this book I will be presenting a traditional [West] African perspective on the topic of erotology, as I have already discussed the religious perspective of this topic in my book, *A Taste of Honey: Sexuality and Erotology in Islam.* In this book I will largely be making use of the opinions and findings of the traditional African and Arab erotologists in their discussions about erotology.

In order to refine this work and make it more relatable to the modern day reader I have supplemented the advice of the erotologists with some words of wisdoms found in the works of prominent contemporary writers in the field of male-female relationships. These include writers such as, Tariq Nasheed (*The Art of Mackin'*),[3] Robert Greene (*The Art of Seduction*), David Deida (*The Way of the Superior Man*), Lou Paget (*How To Give Her Absolute Pleasure*), and Alex Comfort (*The Joys of Sex*).

---

[3] *Mackin* which Nasheed purports is based upon Eastern philosophy and culture. According to Nasheed, the East refers to Africa, ancient India, Chinese and the Middle East. The "mackin' game" is about integrity and self-worth, positive mentality and confidence. It is mainly geared to psychological gratification as opposed to physical gratification like the classical erotology works.

To be honest I am quite surprised that there aren't more books about the joys and dangers of womanising from a male perspective, especially as a large number of men that I know have womanised at some stage in their lives.[4] I felt an honest presentation about the realities of this issue should be discussed. Rather than pussyfoot around the topic of womanising, I will be speaking frankly about some of the pleasures and pitfalls that can occur as a result of reckless womanising which should serve as a lesson for us all.

The Rules of Engagement

First, you have to learn the rules of the game. And then you have to play them better than anyone else.

Every game has rules. The game of sexual love is no different. Men and women play the same game but with different rules. Men are wired to primarily seek physical gratification (sex) from women, whilst women primarily seek emotional gratification (love) from men. This does not mean that men do not desire emotional intimacy or that women are not interested in physical stimulation. We are just different in our approach and what we find more important. The breakdown of communication and understanding in this field is the

[4] There have been a number of American films which have explored the issue of womanising from the perspective of an African descendant male, such as; *Shaft* (1971 and 2000), *Hangin' With The Homeboys* (1991), *Boomerang* (1992), *Def Jam's How To Be A Player* (1997), and *The Brothers* (2001). It is interesting to note that the portrayal of black womanisers differs from white womanisers as depicted in films such as; Dr. No (1962 and the other 007 James Bond films), *Alfie* (1966 and 2004), *The Pick-Up Artist* (1987), *What Women Want* (2000). The approach, style and intent of the womanisers differs in the films, where the black womaniser is stereotypically portrayed as being a smooth, sweet-talker, disciplined man who is having fun with his female lovers. In contrast, the white womaniser is often portrayed as being immature without moral restraint, but secretly desires "true love" to curb his womanising ways.

cause of heated arguments, physical altercations, and marital breakups. It is a never ending debate which is very unlikely to come to an end anytime soon.

Rather than trying to speak on behalf of both genders that have their own perspectives and cultural biases, I will be speaking from a male point of view. My West African cultural upbringing and religious beliefs has undoubtedly shaped my opinions and views on this subject, as has my own personal experiences, which unfortunately, have not always been in conformity with my religious and cultural ideals. Nevertheless, life experience with women from various backgrounds has provided me with an insight into this topic which I most likely would not have obtained otherwise.

Personally, I am surprised how many men do not take the time to try and understand women, let alone satisfy them. Unfortunately many women, both married and unmarried, are sexually frustrated and have unsatisfying sex lives due to male laziness and ignorance of erotology (the art of sexual love and lovemaking). I hope that this book may help solve this problem and can provide some benefit to the reader.

Acknowledgements
I want to thank my father who taught me the principles of manliness, the erotologists who preceded me, and the women of quality who were the source of inspiration behind this book. Special thanks must go to my older brother, Azeez Akande, for this valuable insights and contribution. I also have to thank God for not being the reckless individual that I used to be. To Allah, and Him alone deserves all praise.

Habeeb Akande

INTRODUCTION: THE ART OF SEXUAL LOVE

Sex is the greatest pleasure given to man.[5]

An art is a subject of study that is primarily concerned with human creativity and social life, such as languages, literature and history (as contrasted with scientific or technical subjects). Another definition of art is that it is a skill at doing a specified thing, typically one acquired through practice. Sexual love is a deep feeling of sexual desire and attraction. It can also be used to refer to sexual activities (often including sexual intercourse) between lovers.

Erotology

There is no shame in [sexual] knowledge.
(Arab aphorism)[6]

Erotology is defined as the study of sexual love and lovemaking. It is also defined as the study (or art) of sex as a skill. Etymologically, it is derived from the Greek word '*eros*,' meaning passionate love, and the suffix 'ology' meaning a 'subject of study' or 'a branch of knowledge.'

The study of sex and sexuality can be traced back to ancient Greece from the works of Hippocrates, Plato and Aristotle. Some historians have said that the

[5] Statement was said by an unknown erotologist. Newman, 2014, p. 41
[6] An aphorism is a terse saying embodying a general truth. The Arab aphorism is similar to the popular proverb, "There is no shame in not knowing, the shame lies in not finding out."

oldest handbooks on sex are in fact from the ancient Chinese. Three erotological works were found among fourteen Taoist medical manuscripts in a tomb in Hunan province in 1973. According to historian Louise Foxcroft:

> [In] these writings, sexual satisfaction was deemed paramount because of the mystical benefits, good health and pleasures it bestowed, as long as it was enjoyed according to certain theories that didn't undermine individuals and society.[7]

In ancient times sex was considered to be a sacred duty and part of the natural order, where there was no link between eroticism and sin. Men were also advised to have sex with as many women as possible, but they should always be sparing with their *qi* (energy).

Arguably the most prominent work in antiquity on the subject of *eros* is Plato's *Symposium,* which is a discussion among the students of Socrates on the nature of *eros.* Ancient Indian philosopher Mallinaga Vatsyayana's third century erotic manual *Kama Sutra* (Treatise of Pleasure) is generally considered the standard book on erotology. The *Kama Sutra* is a religious erotological treatise written to advise people about the ethics and art of sexual love from a Hindu perspective. *Ananga Ranga* (Stage of Love), is another erotological text, written by the Indian writer, Kalyana Malla, in the fifteenth or sixteenth century. Kalyana Malla's love manual is often compared to the *Kama Sutra,* on which it draws. The introduction of *Ananga*

[7] Foxcroft, 2014, p. 10.

Ranga speaks about the importance of studying erotology:

> It is true that no joy in the world of mortals can compare with that derived from the knowledge of the Creator. Second, however, and subordinate only to this, is the satisfaction and pleasure arising from the possession of a beautiful woman. ... And thus all you who read this book shall know how delicious an instrument is a woman, when artfully played upon; how capable she is of producing the most exquisite harmony; of executing the most complicated variations and of giving the divinest pleasures.

Ancient Greek philosophers Galen and Soranus further advanced and systematised ancient Indian sexual knowledge, which later motivated Arabic speaking Muslim and Christian writers to write extensively about the "art of coition" (*ilm al-bah*) literary genre and the spiritual joys of physical ecstasy. The influence of ancient Indian and Greek philosophy in the development of the [Islamic] art of coition literary genre is evident by the Arabic speaking erotologists' numerous references to Indian and Greek physicians and philosophers in their treatises.[8]

Erotology in the Middle East and Africa

The Arabic speaking erotologists not only assimilated the ancient Greek theories in their works, but they expanded and developed upon them.[9] Where Arab erotological texts excelled was in the use of language in their description of the art of lovemaking. Classical

[8] Newman, p. 28.
[9] Newman, p. 32.

Arabic is rich in its use of rhetoric and sexual euphemisms which the Arabic speaking erotologists made frequent use of in vividly describing the joys of sexual pleasure.

The Arabic speaking erotologists were predominately Muslims, though there were also some Christian erotologists living amongst the Muslims in the Middle East and Northern Africa. The art of coition erotological literary genre is made up of four sub-genres, (sexually-arousing themed, medical-themed, philosophy-themed and traditionalist-themes erotological works).

The Arabic erotological corpus runs the full gamut of sexuality and erotology, generally combining *ars amatoria* (erotic art) and *scientia sexualis* (science of sexuality): types and positions of lovemaking, beauties of women, Divine rewards, glossary of sexual terms, male and female attractive qualities, aphrodisiacs, penis sizes, types of vaginas, sodomy, lesbianism, pederasty, cunnilingus, anilingus, impotence, nocturnal emissions, voyeurism, hymen restoration, prostitution, bestiality, fetishism, and so on. Some topics were covered more than others.

The Womaniser vs The Sodomiser

A reoccurring feature in many of the Arabic erotological texts was a satirical debate between womanisers (vagina-lovers) and sodomisers (anus-lovers), where they would argue about which organ provides greater pleasure; the vagina or the anus.[10]

---

[10] See *The Pleasures of Girls and Boys Compared* by al-Jahiz, 2002 (translated by Jim Colville), pp. 202-230; and Chapter 2 – "The Beauties of Women and Explaining Their Superiority Over Young Boys," in *The Beauties of Women*, by Andalusian Ahmad ibn Ahmad ibn Hisham. Ibn Hisham, [no year of publication], pp. 19-20.

The debates often took place between a fornicator (womaniser) and pederast (sodomiser). The fornicator was a lover of women and would boast about the joys of female pleasure and the pederast, a lover of young adolescent boys, would put forth his argument for the pleasure of males. The satirical debates contained humorous anecdotes and moral undertones in which the erotologist would conclude on the supremacy of the vagina over the anus as the sexual organ providing greater pleasure.

Citing religious texts and verses of poetry to support their arguments, the "two sinners" would argue which of their vices was the most heinous from a religious and cultural perspective. The fornicator would argue that sodomising boys is not only a transgression against the Sacred Law, but it is also a transgression against the natural order of life. By the end of the debate, the fornicator was usually victorious, and would admit that although his sin was also abhorrent in the eyes of God, sodomising boys cannot be compared to fornicating with multiple women.

I would rather be a womaniser than a sodomiser!

Though many of the erotological texts disapproved of anal sex and same-sex relations, they were not composed to incite violence. Despite the fact that homosexuality was never considered a legitimate sexual practice from a religious perspective in traditional Arab societies, homosexuality appears to have been widely practiced amongst some Arabs which was what prompted many of the erotologists, such as ninth century Afro-Arab scholar al-Jahiz and fifteenth century Andalusian[11] scholar Ibn Hisham, to discuss this issue. The desire for young boys was such an issue that religious edicts were given by Arab scholars warning men about the perils of young boys and sodomy. Unfortunately many non-Muslim Western writers have tried to attribute the homosexuality which occurred in some Arab-Muslim societies to the religion of Islam. Some scholars attributed the widespread phenomenon of homosexuality in Arabia to the Persians and the ancient Greeks, which was said to have greatly influenced Arab culture during the Abbasid era between the eighth and sixteenth century. Mohammad Khalil writes:

> Homosexuality spread in the Abbasid period like a disease till it became a worrying phenomenon, when libertine poets talked about it openly.[12]

In contrast to the widespread practice of male lust for young boys in Europe and the Arab world, the same phenomenon did not exist in sub-Saharan Africa. Historically, sodomy and homosexuality have never been publicly tolerated or accepted in Africa due to the continent's strong religious and culture beliefs abhorring the practice. Anti-gay sentiment is still rife in the majority of African nations today where sodomy and homosexuality is *"unafrican, ungodly and unethical"*[13] according to many Africans. African sexual

---

[11] Andalusia is a region in the south of the Iberian peninsula (modern day Spain and Portugal) that was controlled by the Muslims between the eighth and fifteenth century.

[12] Khalil, Mohammad, "An Unknown Aspect in the Life of Al-Jahiz" http://www.qsm.ac.il/ArbLanguage/docs/majalla/1/2-eng-khalil.pdf

[13] Gambian president Yahya Jammeh said in an interview with Press TV about homosexuality in Africa. (December 2014). http://www.presstv.com/detail/2014/12/01/388256/gambia-raps-eu-pressure-on-antigay-law/

morality remains consistent throughout much of the continent - men are for women, and women are for men. Sodomy and homosexuality is also illegal in many African countries despite pressure from Western countries to legalise same-sex relations.

In 2014, after enacting an anti-gay bill, Ugandan President Yoweri Museveni said that the West should not force its beliefs about sexuality and sexual practices onto Africans:

> Respect African societies and their values. If you don't agree, just keep quiet. Let us manage our society, then we will see. If we are wrong, we shall find out by ourselves, just the way we don't interfere with yours.[14]

Though controversial in the West, Uganda's bill, like Nigeria's anti-gay bill, is widely supported by Africans who regard sodomy and homosexuality as an abomination. Africa's anti-gay laws reflect the beliefs and orientation of the vast majority of African people, whether they are Muslim, Christian or pagans.

Sodomy and homosexuality is viewed as foreign concepts and colonial imports to sub-Saharan Africa. It is seen as a "white man's [sexual] practice" by many black Africans who are resisting the West's attempts to impose its sexual values upon the rest of the world.

No matter to what extent the era has become a white man's era, one cannot take one's own sister as a wife. (Yoruba proverb).[15]

---

[14] http://edition.cnn.com/2014/02/24/world/africa/uganda-homosexuality-interview/

[15] Proverb means that there are some values and habits that will survive the strongest foreign influences Owomoyela, 2005, p. 305.

Eastern Erotology and Western Sexology

As the erotology tradition in the East started to decline in the seventeenth century, a new science dedicated to the study of human sexuality (*scientia sexualis*) arose two centuries later in the West. In nineteenth Europe, the 'Age of Enlightenment' ushered in a vigorous and increasingly secularised discussion of sexual ethics and produced the first program of public and private sex education as well as new classifications and documentations of sexual behaviour. The concept of a theoretical scientific and scholarly effort devoted to sex was first proposed by the Berlin dermatologist Iwan Bloch (d. 1922), who also coined the new term for it: *sexualwissenschaft,* literally translated as sexual science but better translated as sexology.[16] Bloch is widely considered as the father of sexology.

German physician and sexologist, Magnus Hirschfeld (d. 1935), who founded the Institut *für* Sexualwissenschaft (Institute of Sexology) during the years of the Weimar Republic is also credited as being the father of sexology. After Bloch and Hirschfeld, Albert Kinsey (d. 1956) is arguably the next most influential person in the field of sexology.

Often used interchangeably with sexology, erotology differs from sexology in a number of ways. Proponents of sexology argue that sexology is an objective and scientific study of human sexuality whereas erotology, they argue, is subjective and without scientific proof.

---

[16] The term was first translated as "sexual science," but this is somewhat misleading, since the German *Wissenschaft* comprises both the natural sciences and the humanities. The translation as "sexology" is therefore preferable, because the Greek root *logos*, which is part of the word, traditionally refers to all powers of reason and therefore to any rational study, to organized knowledge of any kind. Thus, the Latin-Greek hybrid "sexology" simply refers to the theoretical study of sex, just as the German original.

It can be argued that erotology is actually a greater discipline than sexology as it consists of both the 'subjective' and 'objective' study of human sexuality. Erotology encompasses the [sexologists'] scientific research related to sexual studies as well as the sacred knowledge, morals and ethics found in religious and philosophical texts.[17]

The publication of British biologist Alex Comfort's (d. 2000) landmark illustrated sex manual, *The Joy of Sex: A Gourmet Guide to Lovemaking* in 1976 was an important contribution to human development and sexology in the Western world. *The Joy of Sex* is said to have taken the Western world from an era of "silence and shame about sexuality to one of greater openness and discussion."[18]

In his follow up book, *More Joy of Sex: A Lovemaking Companion to The Joy of Sex;* Comfort said that the prudish attitude of white Europeans prevented them from excelling in the art of lovemaking like black people, which he wanted his (primarily white) readers to learn:

> Where black people of both sexes undoubtedly do score sexually is that Black culture has never lost its body sense as White [people] has and isn't physically uptight. Its body language is much freer and accordingly many black

---

17 http://www.kinseyinstitute.org/resources/sexology.html Classical erotological texts such as Kama Sutra and The Perfumed Garden are a collection of wisdoms, anecdotes and poems which the author has collected or borrowed from the works of his predecessors. Many of the erotologists were editors as much as they were authors presenting original material. The gathering of works from various erotologists gave their works a level of depth that is generally missing from sexologists' studies, which generally focus on scientific topics.

18 http://www.nytimes.com/2000/03/29/us/alex-comfort-80-dies-a-multifaceted-man-best-known-for-writing-the-joy-of-sex.html

> people are better at sex than anxious Wasps [White Anglo-Saxon Protestant] [19] for the same reason that they dance much better. Some degree of soul, rhythm, and body sense is something we others [i.e. white people] need to relearn.[20]

African and Arab Traditionalists

Long before the white man came, we were wearing clothes.[21]
(Yoruba proverb)

A traditionalist is someone who adheres to tradition, especially in cultural and religious beliefs. Tradition is the passing down of elements of a culture from generation to generation, especially by oral communication. In the context of erotology, the traditionalist-themed erotology sub-genre treatises which emerged in the ninth century were pietistic attempts from Muslim writers to educate and at times entertain their readers of the Divine blessing of sensuality from a religious perspective.

The first erotological treatise that is said to have been written in Muslim world was written by the ninth century Afro-Arab writer, al-Jahiz. Since al-Jahiz's work, a number of African and Arab traditionalists have written erotological treatises. Four of the leading African and Arab erotologists, (al-Jahiz, Ibn Falita, Jalal al-Din al-Suyuti, and Muhammad al-Nafzawi) and their treatises will now be presented.

---

[19] Wasp refers to an upper or middle-class white Protestant individual, considered to be a member of the most powerful group in society.
[20] Comfort, 1987. "More Joy of Sex vol. 2," p. 91, in *The Complete Joy of Sex*
[21] Owomoyela, 2005, p. 219.

Al-Jahiz (d. 869)

Abu Uthman Amir Ibn Bahir al-Jahiz was a prolific prose writer and author of works on literature, philosophy, theology, politico-religious polemics and erotology. Born in Basra in 776, al-Jahiz was of African and Arab origin, and a very controversial figure. According to Jim Colville, the first independent treatment of sex in Arabic literature was al-Jahiz's ninth century treatise, *The Pleasures of Girls and Boys Compared.* Al-Jahiz also wrote other erotological treatises; *[Treatise] On Women* and *Book of Marriage and Newly-weds.*[22]

In his erotology treatises al-Jāḥiz generally followed the methodology of the erotology-philosophers, as opposed to the erotology-traditionalists,[23] in its composition in which more emphasis is placed on logic and rationality than on the sacred texts in discussing matters like love, desire and the nature of the soul.

Ibn Falita (d. 1331)

Aḥmad ibn Muhammad ibn 'Alī, known as Ibn Falita, wrote *An Intelligent Man's Guide to Dalliance with The Beloved* almost half a century after the fall of the Abbasid Caliphate in Baghdad. Ibn Falita was also a poet in addition to being a scholar and erotologist.

Ibn Falita's short treatise deals with lovemaking techniques without reference to sexual prescriptions or aphrodisiacs. The purpose of the book, according to

---

[22] Professor Daniel Newman said the oldest known work of erotology may have been written in the late eighth to early ninth century by Persian-born writer, Ibn Bukhtīshū'. See David Newman, 2014, *The Sultan's Sex Positions: Arab Aphrodisiacs in the Middle Ages*, Saqi Books: London.

[23] The traditionalist erotology treatises which emerged in the ninth century were pietistic attempts from Muslim writers to educate and at times entertain their readers of the Divine blessing of sexuality from an Islamic perspective. See *A Taste of Honey: Sexuality and Erotology in Islam.*

Ibn Falita, was to focus on the pleasures of intercourse rather than deal with the medical issues that provide remedies for sexual performance problems.[24] Ibn Falita stresses physical and tempermental compatibility between a man and his wife as well as highlighting matters of health and personal hygiene. Ibn Falita recognises the importance of arousal through foreplay, sexual pleasure for both partners and the female orgasm. Ibn Falita defends the noble purpose of his book in its introduction:

> Which contain a variety of arts which ignorant people would accuse me (the author) of having practised and which intelligent people would be fair enough to believe that I could not have practised. In answer to such a groundless accusation I would say that wine, for instance, has so often been described by chaste people who have never drunk it and have never been condemned for drinking it but who could, with strong observation and clear mind, give surpassing descriptions of it. Of this particular point I would say:
>
> *"Do not be disturbed by a frivolous man*
> *Who is fond of using obscene words.*
> *A man may seem fond of immorality but*
> *Spiritually he may be as chaste as a hermit."*[25]

Sixteenth century, Ottoman scholar Tash Kubri said that Ibn Falīta's book is one of the most comprehensive books on Islamic erotology. The book was translated into English in 1975 as part of a series

[24] Ibn Falita, 1977, p. 5.
[25] Ibn Falita, 1977, p. 5.

presenting classic erotological treatises to English speaking Western readers.[26]

Jalal al-Din al-Suyuti (d. 1505)

Nicknamed the doctor of love, the acclaimed Egyptian erudite Jalal al-Din al-Suyuti is reported to have written at least twenty three treatises on various aspects of erotology.[27] Arguably the most prolific erotology writer in history, al-Suyuti is credited with having written, though the authorship is much disputed, *An Exposition in the Science of Intercourse.* The lithograph begins with the religious cleric exclaiming:

> Praise to the Lord Who adorned the virginal bosom with breasts and Who made the thighs of women anvils for the spear handles of men![28]

According to al-Suyuti, men have an innate desire for women. Commenting on the Qur'anc verse *"Man was created weak,"*[29] Al-Suyuti who was also a leading theologian said the male desire for women is part of his natural disposition and that the weakness the Creator speaks about in the verse pertains to man's sexual weakness for women.[30]

To the same amiable Egyptian polymath are also ascribed *The Blooming of the Jungle in the Knowledge of Sex*, an abstract of his earlier work entitled, *Book of the Scarf on the Benefits of Intercourse.* In a three

---

[26] Translated into English as '*An Intelligent Man's Guide to the Art of Coition*' by 'Adnan Jarkas and Salah Addin Khawwam.
[27] Newman, p. 47.
[28] Al-Suyuti, 1987, p. 1.
[29] Surah al-Nisā' 4: 28.
[30] Al-Suyuti, 2011, vol. 1, p. 165.

volume study of al-Suyuti's erotic works, academic Jūrj Kadr mentioned that al-Suyuti also wrote; *The Sipping of the Pure Water of Lawful Charm, Jungle in the Knowledge of Sex, Halves of the Lemon Regarding the Intricacies of Coquetry* and *Excursion Regarding the Preferences of White, Black and Brown People.*[31]

Like many of his erotological predecessors, al-Suyuti's role was more of an editor and compiler than an original writer. Although al-Suyuti made use of the works of both Muslim and non-Muslim erotologists, he relied upon religious sources as the ultimate source in his investigation.

Muhammad al-Nafzawi (d. 16th century)

Abu 'Abdullah Muhammad al-Nafzawi was a North African, (probably Tunisian) writer of the sixteenth century. Little is known about al-Nafzawi's life. However, he tells us in his preface to his erotological work, *The Perfumed Garden of Sensual Delight* that it was written at the request of the Chief Minister to the Sultan of Tunis after the Minister read al-Nafzawi's previous erotological text, *Illuminating the Performance regarding the Secrets of Intercourse.*

Although, al-Nafzawi addresses *The Perfumed Garden* to his sponsor, the Chief Minister, the intended readership would appear to be a wider audience of uneducated men in the matters of sex. Drawn from previous erotological works from ancient Indian and Arab writers, the stories, jokes and poems in al-Nafzawi's book are written in a simple, populist style and designed to break the ice for his sensitive and unlearned audience. The lists of sexual organs, while

[31] J. Kadr's, 2011, vol. 1, pp. 41-43, Newman, pp. 170-172.

supposed to be illustrative, are clearly intended to amuse as well.[32]

The sexually-charged stories, explicit anecdotes and erotic jokes related in the book have one moral in common, which "brings us to the purpose of the book's composition," Jim Colville states. "They illustrate more or less colourfully, that a wife will inevitably be unfaithful to the husband who neglects her sexually or whose sexual performance is not up to the mark." According to al-Nafzawi, it is sex that holds a marriage together and it is a husband's responsibility to ensure that his wife is sexually satisfied.[33]

A great marriage requires great sex!

Despite *The Perfumed Garden*'s controversial reputation and tattered history in many Muslim countries, al-Nafzawi's short book appears to have been written for a noble religious purpose. It is a prescription to prevent marital breakdown on sexual grounds. The Chief Minister, who was also a Muslim, anticipated the negative reaction that the book might receive when he remarked to al-Nafzawi:

> Everything you have written is true and no-one can take issue with it. You may not be the first to have dealt with this subject but Allah knows, it's one that needs to be more widely understood. Only an idiot or half-educated fool would laugh at this or shut his eyes to it.[34]

---

[32] Al-Nafzawi, 1999, p. x.
[33] Al-Nafzāwī, 1999, p. xi.
[34] Al-Nafzāwī, 1999, p. 4.

The Structure of the Book

In this modern rendition of the traditional literary genre of erotology from an African perspective, I have followed the composition of classic Afro-Arab erotology treatises like *The Perfumed Garden.* For the book's style I have also tried to follow the style and easy-to-read language of the traditional Afro-Arab love genre treatises that were written between the ninth and sixteenth centuries.

The book is arranged in short chapters – eleven in all – to enable the reader to easily find the topic that he requires. Where appropriate, I have included some practical advice and tips on the art of sexual love and lovemaking which the reader can derive benefit from. In this exposition of womanising and erotology, I will discuss each of the arts of sexual love and lovemaking very briefly in order not to bore the reader. In addition to summarising the various branches of erotology that I found in the works of the early erotologists, I have also included some branches on the art of lovemaking that I feel are relevant for the modern day reader.

CHAPTER 1: THE ART OF MANLINESS

Glaring wildly is not indicative of manliness.[35]
(Yoruba proverb)

Manliness refers to the traditional male quality of being brave and strong. Manliness also refers to the fact of being typically male and masculine. Some manly qualities are; courageous, loyalty, confidence, resilience, integrity, personal responsibility, self-reliance, and generosity. An essential virtue of African and Arab manliness is virility – the quality of having a strong sex drive. Virility is regarded as a praiseworthy quality in African and Arab culture as it enables a man to satisfy his women.

Virtue

The worth of a man lies in what he does well.
(Al-Jahiz)[36]

Virtue is a behaviour showing high moral standards. It is a quality considered morally good or desirable in a person. Virtue is also defined as conformity of one's life and conduct to moral and ethical principles; uprightness, and rectitude.

Liberate the minds of men and ultimately you will liberate the bodies of men.
(Marcus Garvey)

[35] Owomoyela, 2005, p. 43. Other variants of the Yoruba proverb states: "Much gesticulation does not prove manliness," "Frowning and fierceness do not prove manliness."
[36] Al-Jahiz, 2002, p. ix.

Virtue of Manliness

In traditional African and Arab culture, manliness is venerated. Males are taught from a young age the importance of manliness, by their fathers, and other male role models who have a strong masculine essence. African and Arab societies are essentially patriarchal where men are taught to be leaders and masters of women. During adulthood, males and females play their respective traditional roles necessary for upholding the norms of the society.[37]

The concept of manliness in African and Arabian culture should not be confused with misogyny (hatred of women)[38] or male chauvinism (the belief that men are inherently superior to women). Manliness in African and Arab culture means a man should treat women with respect and honour, but not be her subordinate.

The modern concept of masculinity in the Western world is very different to the traditional concept of masculinity from the East. The traditional male is an endangered species where there is a loss of traditional male virtues. Speaking about this issue will often result in you being accused of being "misogynistic," "chauvinistic," "sexist," and "anti-women." Do not pay any attention to such nonsense. The importance of being a man of virtue cannot be underestimated, particularly in today's society, with the emasculation and effeminisation of the modern man.

When a man is truly a man, it makes a woman comfortable to truly be a woman.

---

[37] Alaba, 2004, p. 10.

[38] Misogyny is also defined as the dislike of, contempt for, or ingrained prejudice against women.

Values

Values are principles or standards of behaviour. It is also defined as one's judgement of what is important in life. Manliness is about having values. These values should be a set code of conduct, ethics, morals, that he lives by. Often times, these values are governed by religion or cultural traditions.

To be a man of value, is to be a man of worth – a man who provides benefit to those around him. Part of this value comes when a man fulfils his responsibilities as a husband, father and respected member of society.

Men need women as much as women need men. We were created for one another.

Customary Obligations of a Husband

Speaking about the customary obligations for husbands in West Africa, author of *The Sociology of the Yoruba*, N. A. Fadipe states:

> Although a man was not entitled to the earnings of his wife, he was, according to customary usage, held responsible not only for protecting her against assaults and insults, but also for her debts. Cases of shiftless wives who could make no success of their trade and had to be re-started more than once with fresh capital were non uncommon. It was also a man's duty to care for his wife in illness, although the sentiments of kinship have made for the sharing of this responsibility, as well as the responsibility for protection between the

> husband and his wife's close relatives. Yet it remains true that the husband was the person held to be directly responsible for the care of his wife.[39]

Men Appreciates, Women Depreciates Over Time

What this means is that men tend to increase in value over time as he obtains wealth, status and wisdom whereas women tend to decrease in value over time due to weight gain, loss of youthfulness and age.

For example, a young woman at twenty years of age and in the prime of her attractiveness will have many male suitors unlike a twenty year old male who has usually not fully matured or established himself financially in order to attract female suitors. In ten years time, the same man and woman at thirty years of age are likely to be in a reverse situation.

Men at thirty are generally more mature, wise and financially secure which will enable to him attract multiple women. In contrast, women of the same age will not have the same number of male suitors as she had when she was twenty because men prefer younger, more attractive looking women. This is the nature of things, though there are some exceptions to the rule.

That being the case, as a young male in particular, you should understand that your situation is not like that of a woman, you do not have a biological clock and your value will increase over time if you conduct yourself in a correct manner. The women you can attract at thirty are not like the women you attract at twenty, who are usually not fully developed, both physically and emotionally.

[39] Fadipe, 1970, p. 89.

Principles of African and Arab Manliness

You should never compromise your manhood to please anyone, not even a woman that you love dearly. Below are some saying and quotes regarding the principles of manliness from an African and Arab perspective:

Put God first.

Be a leader not a follower.

Never put a woman over your mother.

Manliness means taking responsibility.

Do not speak about private affairs for the world to hear.

Keep your standards even when everyone around you is losing theirs.

Choose carefully where you plant your seeds.

Never pay for sexual pleasure.

Leave a woman that is already taken.

Never beg for a woman's attention.

Never hit a woman.

Do not tolerate disrespect.

Minimise public displays of affection.

Two things a wise man never discloses to the public; his money and his women.

Respect is Everything

Respect is a deep admiration for someone or something elicited by their abilities, qualities or achievements.

In traditional African culture, respect is paramount for a man. Respect is an essential part of Africanness.[40] If a woman regularly disrespects her husband, especially in public, he will often let her go without any hesitation. This is because respect for a man is like what love is for a woman. Women require loving treatment, and men require respect.

Respect should not be confused with intimidation or coercion. It is a voluntary form of respect which the woman shows her husband out of reverence because of the way he looks after her, and treats her.

Sayings about Respect

If she does not respect you, she will replace you.

Never compromise your self-respect for sex.

Boys seek attention, men demand respect

How to Value Yourself as a Man

- **Know your worth** - Do not devalue yourself as a man or lose your self-respect for sex. The notion of putting a woman on a pedestal because of her beauty does not exist amongst men who know their value. A beautiful woman may not necessarily be a good woman. And for a

[40] Africanness is a person born, raised or living in Africa. The term also refers to a descendant of Africa.

man to feel that a woman is "out of his league" merely because of her beauty indicates that he does not value himself.

- **Women receive more from sexual encounters than men.** – When a woman has sex with a man of value and means, she can potentially receive his seed which she could live off for a number of years. The importance of the male seed should not be underestimated for a man of worth. As a man gets older, his seed becomes more valuable.

- **Never beg a woman for sex.** You should not give a woman the impression that she is doing you a favour by having sex with her. Sex is about mutual pleasure, she will receive as much joy from your sexual encounter as you.

- **Be a man of integrity.** Do not comprise your principles and beliefs to impress a woman.

- **Maintain your standards** – Do not adopt the a scavenger mentality who thinks that all women are the same, where "sex is sex."

  Sex with an attractive woman of worth is not the same as sex with an unattractive woman who is easily available. Not only is she easy to get but she may carry some sexually transmitted diseases. Many men will settle for an undesirable woman out of laziness. Do not be such a man. Be sexually disciplined. Have shame in your game.

- **Associate yourself with men of value.** Attitudes and behaviour can be contagious, if you regularly associate yourself with men of low standing and morals, their traits could rub off on you.

- **Do not "kiss and tell."** - Insecure men tend to feel a need to brag about their sexual conquests in order to gain approval from other men. If you know who you are and what you have or can do, you will not require such validation from others. Also women will not respect you if you kiss and tell.

- **Develop a 'quality over quantity' mind-set** – Know that a high-quality woman is better than ten low-quality women. A high-quality woman is not only physically attractive but has a good attitude, attractive personality and sound reputation. If you want to attract a high-quality woman you must first be a high-quality man.

Virility

Virility is defined as; the quality or state of a man being virile (possessing a high sex drive and the capacity for sexual intercourse). According to al-Jahiz, Arabs and black Africans possess virility in abundance. African men are "extremely enthusiastic about their women,"[41] al-Jahiz says. As for the Arabs, he praised their "Arab passion" for women.[42] The ninth

[41] Al-Jahiz, 2002, p. 44.
[42] Al-Jahiz, 2002. p. 177.

century writer also lauded the Africans' high sexual potency and ability to satisfy multiple women.

Being a man is about being able to satisfy your woman, both physically and emotionally.

For many Africans, manliness is synonymous with virility. In traditional African culture where men are allowed to have as many wives as they can afford, a man with multiple wives is an indicator of his virility which many Africans take pride in, as it reflects their sexual prowess and ability to sire a number of children with different women.

A man without a woman is like a vase without a flower.
(African proverb)

CHAPTER 2: THE ART OF WOMANISING

"There is no pussy like new pussy."[43]

According to the Oxford dictionary, to womanise is used (of a man) who engages in numerous casual sexual affairs with women (used to express disapproval). Womanising is the fact of having sexual relationships with many different women.

Collins English dictionary defines a womaniser as a man who indulges in many casual affairs with women. Cambridge dictionary's definition of a womaniser is, "a man who womanizes often has sexual relationships with women or tries to get women to have sex with him." A womaniser is also known as; a philanderer, dog, wolf, player, playa, playboy, lady-killer, ladies man, Don Juan, Casanova, Lothario, Romeo, and Mandingo.

Based on the various definitions, a womaniser can be defined as one of the following:

- A man who desires multiple women and has sexual relations with them.
- A man who seduces or attempts to seduce women as a matter of habit.
- A man who has casual sexual relationships with multiple women.
- A confident, successful man with many sexual partners.

---

[43] Crude expression said by womanisers meaning that there is nothing more delightful than sexual intercourse with a woman except for sexual intercourse with another woman.

The term "womanising" is often used in a pejorative sense to express disapproval for philandering men who have sexual relations with women they are not married to. However, the term womanising, according to one of the definitions cited above could also be used to refer to a polygamist or a serial monogamist.

Why Do Men Womanise?

The reasons vary and only a womaniser can ultimately say why he womanises. Some of the common reasons given for why men womanise are; due to previous bad experiences with women, trust issues, to get an ego boost, validation from others, and the effects of a broken home. Although these reasons may be true for some womanisers, they are not the primary reason why many men seem to womanise as Muhammad al-Nafzawi makes mention of in his book *The Perfumed Garden,* concerning the story of Bahloul,[44] the infamous womaniser in ninth century Baghdad.

According to Bahloul, the reason why men like himself womanise is because of two reasons; self-gratification, and mutual satisfaction.

> Women are my speciality. No-one takes the care that I do on the job. In affairs of this world, Madam, man's motives and desires are very different. Some men give and some men take, some men buy and some men sell. Not me. All that interests me is making love,

[44] Bahloul was a court jester who used to amuse the princes and Viziers (high-ranking political adviser or minister) in ninth century Baghdad, Iraq. Bahloul lived during reign of Ma'moun ibn Haroun (812-833), the seventh Abbasid Caliph, and would joke with the Muslim Caliph about his marital problems.

attending to the needs of pussies in distress and satisfying women's thirst![45]

Variety is the spice of life.[46]

Some men also womanise in order to gain more sexual experiences. No woman is the same as another woman and the more options a man has, the more sexual experiences he will inevitably gain.[47] Another reason why men womanise is because they do not feel a sense of responsibility to women he is not married to:

How can a man be unfaithful to a woman he is not married to?

A man may also womanise out of boredom as he may lose interest in his current lady and desire sexual variety. This can occur after intercourse, or due to a change in her attitude, or excessive weight-gain. The woman he was initially attracted to is not the same woman now so he will seek sexual gratification elsewhere. In saying that there are some men who seek sexual gratification from other women but still have a strong desire for their lady.

What is a Womaniser's Objective?

The objective of many womanisers is to sleep with as many attractive women as they can without getting a sexually transmissible infection (STI) or a woman pregnant. For many womanisers, once he has caught a

[45] Al-Nafzawi, 1999, p. 13.
[46] Proverb meaning new and exciting experiences make like more interesting, In the case of womanising, multiple women brings more joy and pleasure to a man's life.
[47] Nasheed, 2009, p. 17.

STI or impregnated a woman, he is likely to end or slow down his womanising ways. For men like this, they did not retire from the game of womanising, rather the game retired them.

Do All Men Womanise?

Not all men womanise, but a high number of men have womanised or at least wanted to "sow their wild oats," and "get the desire [for multiple women] out of their system" at some stage in their life. Many men will go through a period of womanising or at least potentially womanising, in their youth where their hormones are running wild. This is particularly the case for a man who is good-looking and has financial or social power. The temptation of the flesh will be brought to him even if he is not looking for it. As for men who are not blessed with these qualities, they have to become womanisers by effort. Many great men have fallen for the seductive charms of women as it is very difficult to resist, especially for men of power. There is some truth in the statement:

A man is only as faithful as his options.

This does not necessarily apply to all men as there are many monogamous men who have never had a desire to sleep with multiple women, but truth be told, they are the exception.

For a man to never have womanised or desired multiple women at some stage in his life is rare to many men of African descent. Whether it is because of the high levels of testosterone in their bodies, or part of their African culture to have multiple women is something which occurs amongst many black men of African descent throughout the world.

Do Women Understand Womanisers?

Most women will never fully understand the male sexual experience and his desire to sleep with multiple women. It is something that many women have tried to understand but find it very difficult to comprehend as we think differently.

The male sexual experience of being the penetrator is not like the female experience of being the penetrated. The two realities are fundamentally different. The reason for this lies in the sexual roles of the two; the masculine and the feminine. Both roles are equally important in sexual activities but are very different. The male is the giver, and the female is the receiver, both in reality and metaphorically. The penetrator cannot be compared to the penetrated. The experience and feeling of penetrating is a dominant and powerful role whereas the penetrated occupies a subordinate and submissive role. The two roles are diametrically different.

The sexual activity roles also reflect the traditional gender roles in society where a man wants to be the provider for women. For a man, a heterosexual man that is, the thought of being penetrated is abhorrent, whereas for a woman it is a blissful thought. It is not that one is superior to the other, we are just different.

This is also the case when it comes to sex. Men have an innate desire to sleep with multiple women. Whether this is due to theories about the need to procreate (nature), or cultural upbringing (nurture), is debateable. Nevertheless, whatever the cause for the male desire to sleep with multiple women may it, it is something which is part of the male experience that most women cannot and will not fully comprehend.

Is there a Female Equivalent of a Womaniser?

The female equivalent of a womaniser is commonly referred to by derogatory terms such as; "man-eater," slut, or whore. Whilst women may desire multiple men, as much if not more than men, [in general] they do not have the active desire to want to have sexual relations with multiple men. The emotional nature of women prevents them wanting to engage in sexual intercourse with multiple men. As much as women may find a number of men attractive they rarely act out such desires even if they were given the opportunity to do so without anyone knowing. This cannot be the said for many men who are very weak in controlling their sexual desires. Cultural upbringing and societal expectations also plays a significant role in preventing a woman from promiscuity.

As for the women who do have multiple sexual partners, they are exceptions to the rule. Also you will notice that the women who do end up having multiple sexual partners are often emotionally unstable or going through a phase where they are trying to rebel against the "status quo" of male patriarchy or they are acting out of revenge because they were emotionally scarred by a man that they loved who slept with another woman.

Misconceptions about Womanisers

Many of the misconceptions about womanisers are the perceptions by people, largely women, who do not understand womanisers. There are without a doubt many irresponsible womanisers but there are also many womanisers who are truthful and responsible men. The notion that all womanisers are bad usually stems from a misunderstanding of what it means to womanise and how a womaniser actually thinks.

Womanisers generally do not tell people, especially women whom they love about why they really womanise as they feel many women cannot handle the truth.

Some of the most common misconceptions about womanisers are; they are all unfaithful, deceitful, irreligious, objectify women, demean women, that they do not love the women that they are womanising, have not yet found "true love," were hurt as a child, are immature, have strong sex drives, are not good men, uneducated and uncivilised.

Secret Admiration for Womanisers

Many men secretly admire womanisers and seek to aspire to be one if they have not previously experienced having relations with attractive women. It is fascinating for a man who has difficulty having a relationship with one woman to comprehend how a man can have a relationship with multiple women at the same time. The reason for the fascination lies in the astonishment of a womaniser's ability to charm different women at the same time.

Although most women detest womanisers, many are intrigued by their capability to attract beautiful women. It is not uncommon to find a woman who expresses sheer disdain for a womaniser to end up falling for his charm.

Types of Womanisers

The 'lion vs hyena' is a metaphor to describe two types of womanisers and how they hunt women. Lions and spotted hyenas occupy the same ecological niche, where they compete for prey and carrion in the areas which they coexist. They are both hunters and savages, though lions are commonly associated as being hunters, and hyenas as savages.

As is the case with lion womanisers and hyena womanisers, they often operate in the same vicinity in search for women but their behaviour and mind-sets differ dramatically. The lion represents the respected womaniser, he is calm, calculated and measured; the spotted hyena represents the despised womaniser, he is wild, savage and careless.

Lion Womaniser

The lion womaniser is sexually disciplined who adheres to an ethical code of conduct. A strong leader, he is a hunter of high-value women.

Characteristics of a Lion Womaniser

- Has high standards
- Has a quality over quantity mind-set
- Able to control his sexual desires
- Powerful
- Honourable
- Studies and observes women
- Values himself as a man
- Strategic approach
- Sexually confident
- Reserved about his sexual relationships
- Hunts women alone
- Respected by women
- Possesses strong masculine traits
- Leader of women
- Man of principles, integrity, and morals.

Hyena Womaniser
The hyena womaniser is a sexually undisciplined man who tries to have sexual relations with practically any woman who arouses his desires. He has low standards and is mainly led by his sexual desires.

Characteristics of a Hyena Womaniser

- Has low standards
- Has a quantity over quality mind-set
- Unable to control his sexual desires
- Begging women for sexual activity
- Solicits prostitutes
- Pays women for sexual intercourse
- Masturbates and watches pornography
- Puts women on a pedestal
- Lacks sexual confidence
- Frequently indulges in unprotected sex
- Boastful about his sexual relationships
- Chases women in packs with other men
- Sexually harassing women
- Possesses weak masculine traits
- Follower of women
- Man of popularity, trends and immorality

To sum, a lion womaniser is a man who takes pride in attaining a woman through hardwork and effort; a hyena wants the easy option. The lion has the mind-set and attributes of a brave warrior; honourable, respected, and courageous. A hyena has the mind-set and attributes of a dirty rat; deplorable, despised, and cowardly. The lion is led by his principles, the hyena is led by his desires. The lion has sex when he wants, the hyena has sex when he can.

Stages of Womanising

The four stages of womanising are related below:

Stage 1 – This stage is that of a potential womaniser. It describes a man, usually in his teens to early twenties, who has become sexually active for the first time with a woman he has attained through his own efforts but seeks alternatives. After feeling a sense of pride and satisfaction by his first sexual conquest, he desires more sexual experiences. Tariq Nasheed says:

> When a man gets a taste of sex, he wants to know two things and two things only: how to get more women, and how to get better [quality] women.

Despite the desire for multiple women, not every potential womaniser will become a player, either due to inability, or self-imposed restraint due to his religious, cultural or moral beliefs.

Stage 2 – At this stage, the man is more experienced in womanising. He has had a number of physical relationships with women and has reached a level where he has effectively figured out some useful seduction and lovemaking techniques that works well for him.

The mind-set of a womaniser at this stage is "sex is sex," irrespective of the methods of obtaining it and the quality of woman he has sex with. He is unscrupulous and lacks self-restraint, just concerned about his own sexual gratification. Most men under thirty years of age and scavenger (hyena) womanisers are of this stage.

Stage 3 – At the third stage, the womaniser has evolved his game to the level where he is fairly competent in satisfying a woman's physical desires but struggles to satisfy her emotional needs. His lovemaking skills are intact, but he has yet to master the art of mental penetration.

The other type of womaniser at this stage, is the man who has the ability to satisfy a woman's emotional desires but he lacks the ability to satisfy her physical needs. He may be fairly competent in seducing a woman mentally but his physical penetrative skills leaves women experiencing great frustration by his poor sexual performance.

The third stage is the highest level that the average womaniser will reach in his life. This is because the average man, in general, has been taught to value physical stimulation over emotional penetration. Womanisers who excel in mental penetration are rare but those that do, often have difficulties in knowing how to satisfy the physical needs of a woman. A number of womanisers at this stage are like nomadic lions. They are not alpha males yet but they have the possibility to be one.

Stage 4 – This is the last stage of the womaniser, he is like the alpha male lion – the leader of the pack. A man at this stage has excelled in the art of physical and mental penetration. Not only is he well-versed in meeting women's physical desires but he is equally capable of satisfying her emotional desires.

A womaniser at this stage is very dangerous, as he has the capability of causing a great deal of heartache if he acts recklessly. He has attained great power and as the saying goes, "with great power, comes great responsibility."

Dangers of Womanising

The dangers of womanising can result in physical, psychological or spiritual harm. The fear of the harmful consequences which may occur as a result of womanising is the main reason which deters men from doing something that they desire with multiple women. Fear is the strongest and oldest emotion known to mankind. It serves as a powerful motivator to prevent men from danger and resist the temptations of women. Some of the dangers and warnings about womanising are related below:

- Sexually transmitted infections
- Honeytrap and unwanted pregnancy
- Marital and family breakups
- Financial costs of child support and divorce
- Falsely accused of rape[48]
- Breaking a woman's heart
- Attacked by the woman's male family members
- May find it difficult to be faithful in the future
- Lead people astray
- Loss of the woman or women that you love
- Reputational damage
- Shame of sleeping with an unattractive woman
- Illegal in some countries
- Your sexual desire becomes your Lord
- Divine punishment

[48] Some vindictive women will falsely accuse a man of rape after "drunken sex," "regrettable sex," or out of revenge in order to destroy a man's life. Many African-American men are falsely accused of rape in the United States due to the false perception of black men being womanisers and sexual predators.

The wise elders of the Yoruba[49] would try and curb womanising men by advising them about the dangers of over-indulgence in sexual intercourse:

> The big squirrel is eating bananas (bait on a trap,
> The big squirrel is savouring the sweetness,
> The big squirrel doesn't know that it is the sweetest thing that kills the eater!

Another saying from the wise Yoruba elders:

> Womaniser: "I screwed her almost to the point of killing her."
> Yoruba elder, "It is the body of the screwer that will eventually suffer."[50]

Sexually Transmitted Infections (STIs)

Sexually transmitted infections (STIs), also known as sexually transmitted diseases (STDs) are passed from one person through unprotected sex or genital contact. The more a person womanises the higher the chances of catching a STI, especially if the women are promiscuous. The danger of catching a STI is one of the biggest dangers of womanising as some STIs can cause great pain, infertility, and even death.

STIs are considered to be a by-product of lewdness and promiscuity which many of the Arabic-speaking erotologists related, citing the words of the Prophet Muhammad:

[49] Yoruba people are an ethnic group of southwestern Nigeria and southern Benin. Outside of Africa, a large number of Yoruba people are found in the United Kingdom, United States of America and Brazil.
[50] Alaba, 2004, pp. 11-12.

> Never does sexual perversion become widespread and publicly known in certain people without them being overtaken by plague and disease that never happened to their ancestors who came before them.[51]

Sex with women is a great and wondrous thing which cannot be denied, but is something which should not control one's life as it could lead to your destruction as the following sayings and facts inform us:

If you lie down with dogs, you will get up with fleas.

Rumours are like sexually transmitted diseases, both are spread by whores.

Fish in another man's pond and you will catch crabs.

Prevention is better than cure.

The greater the number of sexual partners a person has, the greater the risk of contracting an STI.

The more people drink alcohol the less likely they are to use protection.

Beware of the Honeytrap

Honeytrap, also spelt 'honey trap,' is a scheme in which a woman lures a man into a compromising situation to provide an opportunity for blackmail or harm. A pregnancy honeytrap is a where a woman tricks a man to fathering her child. Deceptive pregnancy honeytraps usually come either by way of a woman stealing sperm to impregnate herself, or by way

[51] Related by Ibn Majah

of misleading her lover into thinking that she is using contraception and is not intending to become pregnant.

Protect your seed.

Many women also honeytrap men into getting married by becoming pregnant by him. This is especially the case for men with wealth and/or status. Some women will target such men and may not set up their honeytrap for years until she has earned his trust. Many women also believe that they can change a man for the better. This is especially the case for a womaniser. Setting up a honeytrap to become pregnant is seen as a way to "help change his womanising ways," so that he can commit to her. Though a very callous tactic, honeytrapping has curbed the womanising ways of many men so that they can fulfil their responsibility of fatherhood.

Some women set honeytraps to have children with men in order to control.

Many career-driven and unmarried women claim that they do not want to be a mother but underneath they desperately want to start a family. The craving for a baby drives some women to the ultimate deception. Many womanisers are oblivious to the honeytrap risk, especially those who are reckless in their philandering ways. If a man wants to avoid any chance of unwanted fatherhood, he should not be so naïve and trusting of women when she says she is using contraception. This is particularly the case for childless women who are over thirty years of age, or women who are very broody.

Some women will resort to any methods to conceive, irrespective of their lover's approval. Piercing the condom and stealing sperm from a used condom are some of the most common honeytraps that women employ in order to conceive. The ticking biological clock plays heavily on women's mind, especially as they age. Many women would also lie about using contraception in order to get pregnant in spite of their partner' wishes.

Too many men underestimate women, especially women whom they are attracted to. Many western women today are used to getting what they want, they believe that "having it all" is their right, not a privilege. This explains why many women who have trapped a man into fathering her child do not feel any remorse for such callous actions. According to many women who think this way, life without a child is seen as a failure, thus prompting many to resort to any lengths to conceive. As a man you should not underestimate the intelligence of a woman. They can be extremely calculated and manipulative. This is the case of all women, as there are many good wholesome women who would never honeytrap a man, but there are definitely a large number of women who will.

False Accusation of Rape

African-American author Dr Boyce Watkins warns men about the perils of womanising in his article, *How Sleeping With The Wrong Woman Might Turn You Into A "Rapist:"*

> My warning to young men is to be extremely careful about how, where and with whom you

spread your seed. The dumb ass[52] music on the radio sends a message that every time a beautiful woman opens her legs for you, you're supposed to "take it." They don't remind you that some of these women may be diseased, and that stripper/jump off/random woman you slept with on a one night stand might possibly end up being the mother of one of your kids.

Even beyond the simple hazards that come with lying down with a woman who could destroy your life in a heartbeat is the fact that some women (not all) are FLAT-OUT-CRAZY. You might think you're in control because she's sweet, sexy and hangs on your every word. But you also run the risk that she may decide to punish you by dropping an ugly allegation that could send your entire life into a tailspin. I won't even talk about how often brothers go broke from paying a ton of child support.

Sex is a wonderful and powerful thing, but with anything that s powerful, there comes a great deal of responsibility. Slinging your "stuff" at any pretty girl who comes along is a great way to end up with a bunch of problems you don't want. Believe me, I've seen it far more times than you can imagine.

The temptations are great and the risks of infection, unwanted pregnancies and false

[52] Original text, stated "a**."

accusations are extremely high for African American men. So, I concluded a long time ago that having whatever you want is not always good for you, and you have to be extremely careful about who you allow into your life.

So, as you enjoy the spoils of being young and the fact that it's easier than ever to get women to sleep with you, understand that all that glitters ain't gold, and you have to respect your body. But even beyond that, respect your future and don't put it in the hands of a stranger. She might be a wolf in freak's clothing.[53]

Can a Man Stop Womanising?

Arguably the greatest challenge a womaniser will face is to curb his womanising habit, particularly if he still is in a position to womanise. Many former womanisers will stop womanising because they are not able to do so any longer, whether due to age, loss of confidence, wealth, status, and/or fame. The real difficulty is when a man decides to stop womanising out of his own volition which is normally done because of a commitment he has made i.e. to a woman in the form of marriage or out of religious sincerity.

Having a father figure or a respected womaniser advising him is an important deterrent to prevent or stop a man from the perils of womanising. To some respect, only a womaniser can really understand the struggle of another womaniser. Not all men are built to be womanisers, so they may think that it is easy to

[53] See Boyce Watkins, "How Sleeping With The Wrong Woman Might Turn You Into A "Rapist.""

stop than it actually is because they have never enjoyed the pleasures of attractive women.

When a womaniser has enjoyed the pleasures of high-quality women, it can be very difficult to be content with women of a lesser calibre. Overcoming womanising can cause great trauma for a recovering womaniser as he may find himself reminiscing about his past exploits and what might or could have been.

Many womanisers will stop their philandering ways once they have attained their goals. Other womanisers who may not have reached their womanising goals will try and overcome the desire to womanise by turning their attention to other pursuits such as recreational activity or business endeavours.

Overcoming womanising for many men is an on-going struggle that may last for the rest of their lives. A man can stop womanising, but it will take strong willpower and Divine assistance. Philandering can be addictive for a persistent womaniser. For some men, the process required to wean a womaniser off women is like a drug addict weaning himself off crack cocaine or heroin. It is a battle which requires strong resolve from within and mental toughness. No one can stop a man from womanising unless that is something he really wants to do. With that said, even the most "reformed womaniser" will continue to desire multiple women. The challenge is how to deal with this desire, particularly when an opportunity to womanise presents itself.

The process to overcome womanising varies amongst men. Some find it easier to overcome than others. The most important thing is that a man acknowledges his errors and tries to a better man going forward as the African-American civil rights leader *Martin Luther King Jr.* famously said, who had a difficult time dealing with the trials of womanising:

> *"I may not be the man I want to be, I may not be the man I ought to be, I may not be the man I could be, I may not be the man I truly can be, but praise God, I'm not the man I once was."*

The Womaniser's Desire for a Challenge

For many womanisers, the prospect of sleeping with only one woman for the rest of his life is a troubling thought. Men in general need challenges in their lives to make life worthwhile and interesting. For womanisers, their challenge happens to be women because of the excitement and enjoyment multiple women brings. The intensity of the gratification of the sexual conquest is only as intense and pleasurable as the difficulty of the challenge. A high-quality woman will often bring a womaniser the most pleasure because she is not easily attainable.

Womanisers tend to be goal-orientated individuals, and once a goal has been achieved, the challenge loses its appeal. Womanising can actually become very boring once a man has achieved his goals or he does not feel that there are any women worth pursuing. Some womanisers' goals are to sleep with a certain number of women, others seek a certain quality of woman. Once they have attained their goal, they can end their womanising ways.

The Pleasure of the Hunt

Many men only get a sense of fulfilment from the effort they put in to a task. This is also the case when it comes to women. The "pleasure of the hunt" or the "thrill of the chase" is an exhilarating experience for some men. Men are happy to chase women as long as they are receptive to it. For many men, half of the fun of hunting women lies in the chase and makes the catch worthwhile. Confident women are desired by men but sexually aggressive women are disliked. This is because the perception of winning a woman over is still very important to men.

To have a woman given to a man without any effort on his behalf can lead to feelings of suspicion towards her as men often times want to be the hunter rather than the hunted. Hunting is part of his makeup as a man. It is part of the competitive nature of men to seek challenges, and for many men, there is no bigger and more pleasurable challenge than attaining a high-quality woman that he desires.

Attracting a High-Quality Woman

Becoming a man of quality is about having a certain mind-set, level of confidence and knowledge. A man of quality has strong principles and embodies traditional virtues of manhood, particularly confidence. He is charismatic but also knows how to satisfy the mental and physical desires of women.[54]

A highly-desirable individual is a high-quality individual. Someone who is highly valued and highly sought after. For a man, a woman is his most prized possession. Men are known to fight and kill over a woman. And the more value the woman is in a man's eyes, the more he will fight and work for her. This is especially the case for a highly desirable (high-quality) woman.

If a man wants a high-quality woman who is not only physically attractive but has a good reputation

[54] Nasheed, 2005, pp. 7-9.

and nice personality, he must be a man of quality. Afterall, quality attracts quality. Every man desires to have sexual intercourse with beautiful women, but beauty alone is not enough to earn the true admiration of a man. The woman has to beautiful and of fine repute to fully earn his admiration.

For example, if a woman is beautiful but is promiscuous or a working-girl,[55] any sexual experience he has with her will be one which he cannot be proud of as he will know that another man can easily have sexual relations with her. A woman's repute (status, reputation, character and morals) is just as important as her physical attractiveness. A woman having the combination of the two, beauty and fine repute, is the type of woman men ardently desire. However such women require a lot of work and effort. If you want to attract a high-quality woman, you must be a high-quality man.

No other animal romances the wife of a lion.
(African proverb)[56]

[55] A "working girl" is a prostitute who sells sexual favours for payment).
[56] Johnson Hodari, 2009, p. 58

CHAPTER 3: THE ART OF ATTRACTION

When a man's penis erects, he can say farewell to two-thirds of his reason.[57]
(Fayyad Ibn Najih)

Attraction is the feeling of sexual desire for someone. It is of two types; physical and non-physical. Attraction is also referred to as emotional stimulation and [sexual] chemistry.

Sexual Desire

Sexual desire is originated from the old French and Latin words *desir* and *desiderare.* In the Oxford dictionary [sexual] desire is defined as "a strong [sexual] feeling of wanting to have something, or wishing for something [sexual] to happen."

Men are commonly believed in traditional African and Arab societies to have stronger libidos than women, which is one of the reasons why they have multiple wives.

African and Arab Polygamy

In traditional African and Arab culture, where polygamy is permitted for men, women are expected to be monogamous. Although adultery is strictly prohibited, adulterous women are chastised more than men as Nigerian Professor of Sociology, Patrick A. Edewor states:

[57] Al-Ghazālī, 2007, p. 23.

> Nigerian culture, as many African cultures, allows or even encourages men to contract polygamous marriage and a man who engages in extra marital relations does not receive general condemnation as a woman does. He might even be privately hailed for his behaviour. On the other hand, not only would such an act by a married [person] receive wide condemnation but would in fact be ruthlessly and severely punished.[58]

In regards to extra marital sexual affairs, the woman is duty bound to be faithful to her husband while the rule is loose regarding the man. In fact, in many traditional African societies, women are expected to be calm when their husbands have been found to have been involved in an adulterous affair. The belief underlying the African custom of polygamy is that the Creator in His wisdom has made it so.[59] Popular Yoruba musician, Ebenezer Obey, reflects such attitudes in one of his songs:

A man can have six wives,[60]
It is not bad.
But to one man only,
God appointed a woman to marry.[61]

The "one man, one wife" Christian concept of monogamy is rejected by many Africans, even some African Christians who have publicly embraced the

[58] Edewor, 2006, pp. 375-376.
[59] Alaba, 2004, p. 6.
[60] In traditional Yoruba culture a man can have as many wives as he can afford. However, in Islam, a man is restricted to a maximum of four wives.
[61] Familusi, 2012, p. 304.

"foreign custom" of monogamy will still have additional wives and/or mistresses in private.

Polygamy is entrenched in the African male psyche as it is considered to be part of his heritage and can also serve as a corrective measure for cantankerous wives who believe that they are without flaws as the Yoruba proverb informs:

A woman who does not yet have a co-wife does not know what disease she has.
(Until one has enemies, one seldom knows one's flaws).[62]

"Double-Standards" in the West

The apparent double standards regarding multiple sexual partners for men and women is also a contentious issue in contemporary Western societies where men are labelled as "studs" if they have multiple sexual partners, and women are labelled as "sluts" if they have multiple sexual partners.

In an article by Paul Elam, founder and publisher of *A Voice for Men Radio*, about this apparent double-standard, Elam said, that men who have a lot of sexual partners are regarded in much more positive terms than women who do the same thing. Though there are some exceptions, in general the social view of promiscuous men and women is fairly consistent where men are lauded and women are deplored.

According to Elam, it is not an unfair double standard as men and women are different. He explains that the reason for the apparent double standard lies in the difference that it takes for men and women to have multiple sexual partners. For a man to have a high volume of sexual partners, he must:

---

[62] Owomoyela, 2005, p. 308.

1) Have great sexual magnetism based on physical appearance, or
2) Have visible economic success, or
3) Significant social status among other men, or
4) An operational understanding of women and their desires and the ability to manipulate those things, or
5) The ability to project high self-confidence in social settings, or
6) A combination of two or more of the above.

As for women, in order to have a high volume of sexual partners, a woman must:

1) Have a vagina.

The reality is that it does not take much for a woman to attract multiple sexual partners, Elam argues. Congratulating a woman because she can attract sexual attention from men is like being in awe of an adult because he can outrun a child.[63]

Women who value their vagina are less likely to want to sleep with multiple men as it will be a form of devaluation in the eyes of other men. A woman who sleeps with a number of men is also looked down upon by women for degrading themselves. As for men, this does not exist to the same degree. Men often admire a man for having multiple women as he is aware of the difficulty of the task.

---

[63] Elam, Paul, "On Studs and Sluts."

Male Desire for Sexual Variety

The male desire for sexual variety varies amongst men but is considered to be part of his natural disposition, relationship author David Deida writes:

> Any man with a masculine sexual essence will desire sexual variety. Even if he loves his intimate partner and is completely committed to her, he will naturally want sexual occasions with other women besides his chosen intimate partner. How a man deals with his desire for other women is up to him. He should know, however, that there is no way to avoid such desires. He should also know that acting on such desires, though temporarily enlivening and exhilarating, often ends up complicating his life far more than the occasion itself is worth.[64]

Female Attractiveness

A woman's greatest asset after her beauty is her natural perfume. It comes from the whole of her hair, skin, breasts, armpits, genitals. The smell and feel of a woman's skin probably have more to do with sexual attraction than any other single feature. – Alex Comfort[65]

A marital partner and sexual partner are two different types of women in the eyes of a man. The qualities, men seek in a marital partner is not the same qualities he is looking for in a sexual partner. For a marital partner, a man will seek the physical and non-physical

[64] Deida, 2004. p. 96.
[65] Comfort, 1993, p. 30.

attractive qualities. However for a sexual partner he is largely concerned about her physical qualities. Some men can tolerate ugliness in a woman but this is rare. For a man, physical attractiveness is incumbent for a sexual partner.

Erotologists wrote a plethora of material on the attractiveness of women, predominately concentrating on their physical qualities.

Ibn Nasir al-Katib related:

> A woman is loved and praised for having the 'four qualities:'
>
> 1. Four black things; [namely her] hair, eyelashes, eyebrows and eyes.
> 2. Four white things; skin complexion, whiteness of the eyes, teeth and armpit.
> 3. Four red things; tongue, lips, cheeks and buttocks.
> 4. Four round things; face, eyes, heels and ankles.
> 5. Four long things; neck, hair, eyebrows and fingers.
> 6. Four broad things; forehead, chest, hips and eyes.
> 7. Four sweet smelling things; nose, mouth, armpits and vulva.
> 8. Four narrow things; nostrils, ears, navel and vagina.
> 9. Four small things; mouth, nose, hands and feet.
> 10. Four thin things; eyebrows, nose, fingers and lips.[66]

[66] Ibn Nasr al-Katib, 1977, pp. 205-206, Ibn Falita,1977, p. 50.

Al-Jāḥiz said:

> A woman should have a good figure, finely chiselled features, a straight back and shoulders. She should have enough flesh on her bones not to be skinny but neither should she be fat.[67]

Ibn Yaḥyā said:

> [The ideal woman has] a well-developed body, a smooth complexion, thick hair, a bright face, a face that looks beautiful without beautification, thin and long eyebrows, black and wide eyes, long eyelashes, a high and a curved nose-tip, a nice mouth odour, bright teeth, a long and a well-developed neck, well-proportioned arms and forearms, a slender waist, broad hips, big buttocks, well-developed legs, a sweet voice, cheerfulness, gentleness, shyness, chastity, devotion, cleverness at handwork and fertile.[68]

A high-quality woman has a combination of five qualities; beautiful face, sexy body, pleasant attitude, well-groomed, and a good reputation.

Egyptian erotologist al-Suyuti related that the best of women is:

The chaste woman who guards her private parts and is sensuous with her husband.[69]

---

[67] Al-Jahiz, 2002, p. 179.
[68] Ibn Yaḥyā.
[69] Al-Suyuti, 2011, vol. 1, p. 145.

Muhammad al-Nafzāwī said:

> There are many different types of women, some of whom are attractive and desirable to men and some of whom are not. For a man, the woman of quality has a full and voluptuous figure, jet-black hair, a broad forehead, arched eyebrows and wide, clear eyes, a moon-shaped face, smooth, soft cheeks, a straight nose and narrow mouth, sweet breath, red lips and a pink tongue. She has a long neck and full throat, broad shoulders and chest with large, firm breasts and a deep cleavage, a neat waist and curved belly with a wide, deep navel, a generous vulva, a soft, tight vagina without discharge or odour – and hot, as if almost on fire – broad hips, firm, ample buttocks, tight curves, firm, strong thighs, long, shapely legs, graceful feet, broad arms and elegant hands. As she walks towards you, she entrances and when she turns around, she's fatal. When she sits, her vulva pouts like a little cupola; lying down, it flutters like a flag does in a gentle breeze and when she stands, it stands majestic like a sceptre.[70]

A slender woman is the joy of her husband on a day of dancing, but a hefty woman is her husband's joy on the day of yams quartered for planting; after she has toted a hundred yam pieces, she walks smartly [towards the farm] ahead of her husband.

(Yoruba proverb meaning good looks are not all that makes a good wife. Good dancers are usually great

---

[70] Al-Nafzāwī, 1999, p. 18.

lovers. The ability to dance seductively with rhythm works well in the bedroom.).[71]

Attractiveness of Large Buttocks

The female derriere is a reoccurring feature in Arab and African discourse on female beauty. A firm, well-rounded, protruding behind is frequently mentioned as being the most desired buttocks form of a woman. Pre-Islamic Arab poets used to metaphorically refer to women as cows as a form of praise because the slow, seductive gait of a woman with large buttocks resembles the nonchalant stroll of a cow from behind. Many of the traditional erotologists lauded women of African descent in particular who were renowned to have a large posterior. Egyptian erotologist al-Suyuti narrated:

> The best of women are those with empty stomachs, large buttocks and large breasts when embraced.[72]

Men who have small members are usually intimidated by women with large-buttocks out of fear that they cannot satisfy them. Historically, women of African ancestry have been ridiculed by Europeans because of the huge size of their derrière. Due to deep-seated sexual insecurities and probably their small members, many European and Asian men cannot appreciate an amply-shaped woman.

Big buttocks wake up an impotent penis.
(Ghanaian proverb)[73]

---

[71] Owomoyela, 2005, p. 223.
[72] Al-Suyuti, 2011, vol. 1, p. 119
[73] Johnson Hodari, 2009, p. 57

Pretty Women with Fine Bodies

A woman who has the combination of a beautiful face and a curvaceous body is a man's delight. Countries which have a large number of pretty women with the finest of bodies can be found in the following four:

- Brazil
- Morocco
- Eritrea
- Ghana

Unattractive Qualities

As for the unattractive qualities which men find in women, al-Nafzawi says:

> The sort of woman men find repulsive is ugly and sullen with matted hair, a protruding forehead and dirty, slit eyes. She has a big nose, wide mouth, bluish lips and wrinkled cheeks, is gap-toothed and sprouts hairs on her chin. The sinews and veins on her wizened neck stick out, her shoulders and chest are narrow and her sagging dugs are leathery. He belly is like an empty basin and her navel juts out like a walnut. Her ribs protrude like bows, her backbone like an iron chain and her buttocks are bony and scrawny. Her vagina is cold and loose, dirty and smelly, lumpy and bumpy and has a discharge. She has knobbly knees, spindly legs, big, flat feet and enormous hands. A woman like that is no good at all, nor is the man who marries her or approaches her. May the Lord protect us from her and her like!

Four Very Unattractive Female Characteristics:

- **The green-eyed monster** is an extremely jealous woman who does not trust men with other women and constantly suspects that her partner is unfaithful due to her own insecurities.
- **The prima donna** is a selfish woman who is only concerned about herself and does not cater to the sexual needs of her man except when she desires.
- **The ingrate** is an ungrateful and unappreciative woman who does not show gratitude to her husband for the good treatment he has shown her.
- **The Nag** is a (nagging) woman who constantly annoys her man to do something by complaining, and talking too much.

  Many women will nag as they are emotional creatures who want to speak about their feelings. The best way to overcome a woman's nagging is to keep calm, be quiet and just listen to her. Also you may need to bite your tongue and look like you care about what she is saying even if she is driving you crazy.

Male Attractiveness

Women desire in men; loyalty, faithfulness, honour, respect, attention, appreciation, affection, love, trust, and great sex!

In the works of the classic erotologists, a large penis was frequently mentioned as the most desirable physical quality which women find attractive in men. As for non-physical qualities, erotologists wrote in more detail about such qualities.

Ibn Kemal Pesha said:

> The characteristics which a woman loves in a man are that he is; generous, courageous, truthful, sweet talker, intelligent, funny, fulfils his promises and responsibilities, understanding, courteous, well dressed, healthy, good mannered and without bodily defects. As well as having many respectable friends, he is not arrogant. That he is broad chested. A man who avoids foolish people and those who are not good. A man who people admire and imitate for his character, clothes and conduct.
>
> The things which attract her to him is that he has clean teeth which he cleans with a toothbrush, fresh breath, clean hands and feet with clipped nails. He wears beautiful clothes and has a pleasant smell. In addition to these characteristics, if he has a lot of wealth and status, he is the most complete and adored man in the eyes of women.[74]

Muhammad al-Nafzāwī said:

> The man of quality should be purposeful and serious, clean and well-groomed, of good build and handsome appearance. He should always speak

[74] Ibn Kemal Pesha, 2010, p. 165.

> the truth and never lie. He should be courageous and generous, with a noble spirit and a gentle heart. He will do what he says and never betrays a confidence or breaks a promise. That is the sort of man women will cherish and desire to be loved and be penetrated by.[75]

Professor Olugboyega Alaba says about male and female attractiveness amongst the Yoruba:

> Attire is a means of expressing sexuality among the Yoruba. Males use various types of *fila* (caps) to demonstrate to their female admirers their elegance; while the females tie their *gele* (head-gears) in various styles to attract the attention of their male admirers. Through the use of adornments, Yoruba males express their manliness.[76]

Unattractive Qualities

As for the unattractive qualities which women find in men, al-Nafzawi says:

> The kind of a man who is repulsive to women is of shabby appearance, ugly to look at and has a small, limp and weedy penis. He is the type who, when he comes to a woman, has no idea how to treat her properly but mounts her without kissing or caressing her, without any sort of foreplay at all. He inserts his flaccid little thing inside her

[75] Al-Nafzāwī, 1999, p.10.
[76] Alaba, 2004, p. 10.

only with the greatest difficulty, jerks once to twice then hauls himself off her, taking longer to do so than he did on the job. His penis then shrivels up and away he goes. He has been described a slow to erect and quick to eject, with a small penis, leaden chest and lightweight buttocks. A man like that is no use to a woman.[77]

[77] Al-Nafzāwī, 1999, p. 31.

CHAPTER 4: THE ART OF THE APPROACH

In certain respects, women are superior to men. It is they who are desired, courted, loved and pursued.
(Al-Jahiz)[78]

The art of the approach is defined as the skill of [a man] speaking to an unknown attractive woman for courtship.[79] To be successful in the art of the approach, a man must possess the following three attributes; confidence, charisma and communication. A man who is well versed in the art of the approach is said to "have game." Having game, or good game for that matter, is the ability of a man to attract women. Good game consists of integrity and honesty and bad game involves deceptiveness and manipulation. Most men do not have game, good game that is, because of a lack of confidence, charisma and effective communicational skills. Though some men are naturally born with these attributes, many others develop them over time with experience, as "experience is the best teacher."

Confidence

Confidence is a feeling of self-assurance arising from an appreciation of one's own abilities or qualities. The essence of the art of the approach is confidence.

---

[78] Al-Jahiz, 2002, p. 173.

[79] Courtship is a period during which a couple develop a romantic relationship, especially with a view of marriage, behaviour designed to persuade someone to marry or develop a romantic relationship with one.

Confidence in a person attracts other people to them, and everyone likes to be around a self-assured individual. This is especially true when it comes to sexual confidence which comes through experience and having a positive attitude.

Sexual confidence can compensate for physical unattractiveness. Some of the most beautiful women in the world are with men who are physically unattractive but they have an attractive and confident personality. It is important to note that there is a difference between confidence and arrogance (overconfidence). There is nothing wrong with being confident, but often times, stupid people will mistake your confidence for arrogance. Women who appreciate you for what you are will admire your sexual confidence as it is a rare trait amongst men.

Tips to Increase Sexual Confidence:

- Success with attractive women will increase your sexual confidence. If you have little experience speaking to attractive women you will struggle to gain confidence.
- Do not overthink what you are going to say before you approach a woman. Rehearsed lines are contrived and attractive women can often detect this.
- Travel outside your habitat. Women in different environments and from different cultures and societies respond differently. There are some women who may not appreciate your approach or charisma so you may need to go somewhere where women will appreciate you.

- Being comfortable in your weaknesses and flaws will help increase self-confidence. You need to be comfortable outside of your comfort zone.
- Do not concentrate on others. If you are mentally strong, you have nothing to fear from other men who may be physically stronger or wealthier than yourself, as the Yoruba proverb states:

A lion does not face peril from a leopard.
(Yoruba proverb meaning that the stronger person has nothing to fear from the weaker person).[80]

Go It Alone

Go it alone is an idiomatic expression to do something by yourself without help from other people. In regards to the art of the approach, it is often best to go and approach a woman by yourself. Many men need to be with their friends to approach women as they lack self-confidence. You should not become dependent upon your friends for courage. Women will respect you more if you have the courage to approach her by yourself. Your friends will not be with you in the bedroom so why do you need their moral support to speak to her?!

Yoruba proverb:

The lizard that fell from atop the iroko tree without breaking its limbs says if no one admires his feat, he will do the admiring himself.
(One should be self-confident enough not to need validation by others).[81]

[80] Owomoyela, 2005, p. 219.
[81] Owomoyela, 2005, p. 203.

Alcohol-Dependency

Many men rely on alcohol, (also known as “liquid confidence,” and “dutch courage,”) or other forms of intoxication to pluck up the courage to approach an attractive woman. Whilst alcohol does increase an individual’s confidence, as well as releasing inhibitions, it causes an individual to lose their sense of perception and control. Approaching a woman whilst intoxicated is not only unattractive to women of quality, but it could also result in a man approaching a woman who he thinks is attractive but is quite the opposite in reality.

As a man you should be in full control of your faculties when speaking to the opposite sex. Alcohol will make you lose this control.

Alcohol provokes the desire, but takes away the performance.

Approach Anxiety

Many men experience nervousness, fear and great anxiety at the prospect of approaching an attractive woman, particularly for the first time. This is known as approach anxiety. As men have historically been expected to approach women i.e. for their hand in marriage, it is incumbent for men to overcome approach anxiety if he wants to attain an attractive woman.

Tips to Overcome Approach Anxiety:

- Stay calm and think of what you can offer her instead of thinking about what she can offer you.

- Gain confidence by socialising more with attractive women in order to develop your interpersonal and confidence skills which will help decrease anxiety.
- Focus on her unattractive qualities if you feel so overwhelmed by her beauty. No woman is perfect and very often the women who appear to be flawless is due to the makeup that she wears. Do not let the facial mask of makeup deceive you into thinking that she is "out of your league" by her physical attractiveness alone. Makeup can be a form of deception as much as it is a beauty enhancement.

The Fear of Rejection

The fear of rejection is another common reason which prevents men from approaching women that they are interested in. Men like to be in control of situations, the fear of women rejecting men plays on men's minds because when he approaches a woman, he is not in control of the situation. The control lies in the hands of the woman. Rejection reinforces self-doubt and insecurities that a man feels about himself. A man needs to overcome this fear if he wants to approach women successfully.

Tips to Overcome The Fear of Rejection:

- If you approach a woman in a respectful and courteous manner, she is more likely to respond in a similar manner even if she were to reject you so it would not cause much embarrassment or pain.

- Remember the worst thing that she can say is no. You will not die if she rejects you!
- Do not pay attention to what people think or say. If your intention is sincere and you want to approach a woman to find out if you are compatible with her, then go ahead. People will always gossip and suspect the worse even if you have good intentions when approaching a woman. Pay them no attention.
- Remember the feeling of regret of a passed opportunity is stronger than the pain of rejection.
- Be bold and confront your fear. Boldness will alleviate your fear. Women can sense fear and will often react negatively to a nervous, unconfident man. However, they will react positively to a confident, self-assured man.

Fear of battle never afflicts a warrior.
(Yoruba proverb meaning one should be bold in pursuing one's goals.)[82]

How to Deal With Rejection?
Knowing how to deal with rejection is very important. Not every woman will be interested in you. Failure is an inevitable part of life. Every man who has been successful with attractive women has experienced rejection before.

The best way to get over a woman is to get under another woman.[83]

---

[82] Owomoyela, 2005, p. 212.
[83] Meaning quickly remarrying after a bitter divorce will ease the pain of the breakup.

- Even if you have the slick approach, it will not guarantee that a woman will be interested in you. Sometimes you might run into a woman who is already spoken for, does not have the time to stop and talk, is having a bad day, or is just not interested. In any case, do not let this get to you and take the rejection personally.
- Think of it as her loss or your gain. Consider it that she has missed out on a good opportunity or she may not be good for you in the long run. Remember, an attractive woman is not necessarily a good woman.
- Self-reflect after rejection to assess where you may have gone wrong so that you can improve your approach technique for next time. It can also make you grow stronger as you can learn from the experience.

Charisma

Charisma is compelling attractiveness or charm that can inspire devotion in others.

Tips to Become Charismatic

- Be the best version of yourself, as the oft-quoted saying goes, "Be yourself, everyone is taken."
- Observe charismatic people and see what it is about their charisma that women are drawn towards. It is very likely that some of their qualities are within you which you need to tap into.
- Maintain and improve your natural attractiveness, i.e. by keeping in shape, keeping

well-groomed, increase your knowledge, and gain more interesting experiences by travelling.

- When a man is a leader, a woman will naturally follow. Women follow men subconsciously, especially when they are in love.
- Have the ability to make women feel comfortable around you in order to gain a magnetic rapport with them.
- Be humorous without being cocky or overly silly.

Communication

Communication is the imparting or exchanging of information by speaking, writing, or using some other medium. There are two types of communication in the art of the approach; non-verbal and verbal communication.

Non-Verbal Communication

- Body Language (relaxed, comfortable and confident demeanour).
- Eye contact (observe the eyes for they are windows to her soul).
- Written communication (text messages, e-mails, poems, and love letters).

Verbal Communication

- Word play (vocabulary, choice of words, and sexual euphemisms).
- Voice tonality (controlled, dominant, and deep).
- Delivery (conversational skills and listening skills).

Tips to Improve Your Conversational Skills

For women, the importance of conversation cannot be understated. Most men are averse to conversing with beautiful women due to a fear of not being able to impress her. Rather than focusing on impressing her, you should think about her impressing you. If you have something meaningful to say and speak about, you would want to engage with her, to see where her mind is at. A beautiful woman is nice but a beautiful woman with brains is something else!

In saying that, not all conversations have to be deep and meaningful; it can be light-hearted and fun. Like with most things, it all depends on the situation and woman you are speaking to. Below are some useful tips to improve your conversational skills.

- Do not rely on corny "pick up" lines.
- There is no set formula to "chat-up,"[84] "chirpse,"[85] or speak to women. It is about technique, strategy and improvisation. You need to know how to adapt your approach accordingly. The more life experience you have, the more things you can converse about.
- Intelligence is attractive to high quality women. Speak about something that she will find interesting.
- Offer a unique perspective when conversing.
- Speak less and listen more to what she has to say. Do not speak about yourself a lot or come across like you are interviewing her.

[84] Chatting-up is a slang term to refer to a man speaking to a woman with the intent of eventually engaging in sexual activity with her.

[85] Chirpsing is a slang term, commonly used in London, to refer to a male speaking to a female that he finds attractive with sexual intent.

- Develop good listening skills, and be attentive to what she is saying to engage with her in a stimulating conversation.
- Practice makes perfect – The more you are exposed to situations with women, the better your chances are to respond appropriately to every situation that arises, in terms of what to say and how to react. Socialising with women of different backgrounds will also give you more interesting things to speak about.
- Read books to improve your vocabulary as this may also help in your conversational skills. Women love to talk and having an engaging conversation can be a way to a woman's heart as Tariq Nasheed advises:

> The key to keeping a decent conversation with a female is to get her to talk about herself.[86] [Nasheed continues] women like to hear smooth, and comforting conversation from men, because it gives them a subconscious sense of relaxation.[87]

Tailor Your Approach

The strategy one adopts in acquiring a wife will not do with regard to money.[88]
(Yoruba proverb meaning what suffices in one situation may not be applicable in another).

Tailor your approach depending on the surroundings and the woman. Sometimes you have to be bold, other

---

[86] Nasheed, 2009, p. 150.
[87] Nasheed, 2009, p. 103.
[88] Owomoyela, 2005, p. 214.

times you may need to be smooth. You may also have to adapt your approach based on her culture. Women from certain backgrounds behave differently to others depending on their cultural customs. In some cultures where it is taboo to speak to an unknown woman in public, you may need to adopt a fast and more direct approach when speaking to her. Alternatively you may need to speak to her through a third party, i.e. another female, a friend, the woman's father or male guardian.

Some women will openly show their interest with affectionate gestures, others by way of eye contact, and others by simply smiling. The onus is on you to understand her responses, as many women, particularly attractive women, will not openly show their interest in a man.

Work Ethic

Anything worth attaining requires hard work and effort. This is also the case when it comes to women. You may have to put in the time to search for quality women, and get to know her, her friends and her family. Laziness will get you nowhere. You have to go and get want you want in life even though it may be difficult or uncomfortable at first, as the following Yoruba proverbs informs:

A domesticated dog does not know how to hunt.
(Pampering kills initiative).[89]

The aftertaste of the bitterleaf is sweet.
(Sweetness and pleasure come after exertion).[90]

---

[89] Owomoyela, 2005, p. 201.
[90] Owomoyela, 2005, p. 200.

The Best Places to Meet Attractive Women

Generally, the best places to meet wholesome attractive women are in normal everyday surroundings, particularly during the day in public places like libraries, shopping malls or on the street. In public places, women will be their normal selves without the defence barriers which they tend to put up in social gatherings, parties or when she is with a group of her friends.

There are countless beautiful women who are not married and are not approached appropriately by men because many men assume that they are already spoken for or they feel that the woman is somehow too good for them.

Finding beautiful women in public places does not cost you anything, though you should look presentable and wear nice cologne at all times, you never know when an opportunity to meet a beautiful woman may present itself. Your future wife may be there if you bother to make an effort.

Tips of what not to do when meeting an attractive woman:

- Approaching her from behind.
- Sexually harassing her.
- Shouting inappropriate comments.
- Staring in a lecherous manner.
- Touching or grabbing without permission.
- Wolf-whistling and catcalling.

CHAPTER 5: THE ART OF VERBAL FOREPLAY

All really great lovers are articulate, and verbal seduction is the surest road to actual seduction.
(Marya Mannes)

Foreplay is sexual activity that precedes intercourse. Verbal foreplay can be subtle or it can be direct, sometimes sweet words are required, at other times more explicit terms are needed. Words are a woman's weakness, thus making verbal foreplay a powerful tool to help a man attain her sexual love.

Word Play

Massage her ego with nice words.

Your verbal skills are your most trusted weapon with women. Women love to be teased and complimented to prepare them for penetration and there is no better way to play with women than with your words. A sweet-talker can make a woman moist by his words alone. You should not underestimate the power behind words in the art of verbal foreplay.

Compliments

Compliments, praise and loving words allows a woman to blossom sexually, as author of *The Way of the Superior Man*, David Deida said:

> The masculine grows by challenge, but the feminine grows by praise. A man must be unabashed and expressed in

> his appreciation for his woman. Praise her freely.[91]

Female sex therapist Lou Paget said:

> Women blossom under attention and complimentary comments about their bodies. Most women, even beautiful women with wonderful physiques, question their attractiveness and often have negative feelings about their body image.[92]

However, you should bc carcful with giving a woman too much attention and compliments as she may become disinterested and not appreciate it as Tariq Nasheed advises:

> Attention for a woman is like an orgasm for a man, you can't give it to her too soon.

Treat her like a princess when she behaves like royalty

Sexual Euphemisms

A sexual euphemism is the substitution of a mild, indirect or vague sexual expression for one thought to be offensive, harsh or blunt. Sexual euphemisms are used when referring to sexual matters which are often considered to be unpleasant or embarrassing. An example of a sexual euphemism is the expression "making love" for "having sexual intercourse."

In Yoruba culture, like many other African societies, verbal expressions of sexuality come, as a

[91] Deida, 2004. p. 61.
[92] Paget, 2010, pp. 61-62.

rule, in the form of euphemisms. The names of the sexual organs are rarely mentioned explicitly. For instance, the female sexual organ is referred to as "the eye of a woman's body," while the male organ is called, "a man's thing."[93]

Amongst friends of the same gender, men tend to use more explicit and crude terms when speaking about sexual matters, whereas women tend to use more subtle expressions when referring to sexual matters. Examples of common descriptions used by men for having sexual intercourse are; "fucking," "bust a nut," "hit and run," and "beating." Women on the other hand tend to use subtle euphemisms when speaking about sexual relations i.e. "dating," "seeing each other," "sleeping together," and "making love."

Women desire sexual relations as much as men but can be easily turned off by explicit sexual terms which they feel are inappropriate. Thus, you will need to ensure that you use appropriate language that she is comfortable with. Do not speak to her about sexual matters as you would speak to your male friends about sexual relations and her genitalia, i.e. use euphemistic expressions like "vagina" instead of "cunt" or "pussy," depending on the situation. However, it is important to know your woman. Some women like hearing "dirty" and "naughty" terms to become aroused. Even good girls like to misbehave from time to time.

Tips for Effective Word Play:

- Insinuate your intent with sexual euphemisms.

---

[93] Alaba, p. 11.

- Use humour to make her laugh. Many women are attracted to men who can make them smile or laugh.
- Make use of compliments and affectionate nicknames. The more a woman is complimented, the more it will make her feel sexy and attractive.
- Take a few moments to observe her, before making a compliment that is unique to her.
- Some women find a good conversation more erotic than sexual talk or actual foreplay. Speak to her about anything besides sex but in a slow, deep tone to arouse her hidden desire.
- Explain in detail how you are going to make love to her, do not use language that is crude or too explicit. For example you can use the words; "touch," "caress," "hold," and "penetrate," instead of more explicit and harsher words that you may be thinking but should not always say. Remember a woman is still a woman, she needs to hear delicate words to get her in the mood, particularly if you are not communicating face to face.
- Avoid profanity and speaking about her genitalia all the time. There is a time and place for everything. Even if you want to have intercourse with her, you should not come across as desperate, it will turn her off. You need to stir up her desire to the extent that she is the one who eagerly wants you to penetrate her and not the other way around.
- Tell her how you feel without being over the top.

- If you have had any intimate dreams about her, feel free to let her know, it will make her feel special that you have been thinking about her.

Voice Tonality

It's not what you say, it's how you say it.

A strong presence and a confident voice commands a woman's attention. The voice of a man alone can be the difference between winning and losing a woman's attention. How you speak to a woman determines how she will respond to you.

In terms of voice tonality, there are two types; dominant and submissive. Dominant voices connote leadership, assertiveness and security. A dominant voice will earn you her respect, trust and attention. Submissive voices connote uncertainty, passiveness and self-doubt. A submissive voice indicates that you are seeking approval or validation from her.

Tips to Improve Your Voice Tonality:

- Speak in a deep tone
- Speak slowly
- Speak in a controlled and measured voice

Delivery

Practice makes perfect

With verbal foreplay, it is not only important to be proficient in your word play and voice tonality but in your delivery. There is a time and place for everything and that is the case with the delivery of the words that you utter when conversing with a woman.

Tips to Improve Your Delivery Skills:

- Uttering sweet words alone is not enough, to arouse her desire. It should be said sincerely to have an impact on her heart.
- Tell her about things that you love about her, paying particular attention to the small things as they are often what matters most to women.
- Whisper seductive words in a deep controlled voice prior to actual penetration to increase her sexual desire.
- Some women like when you speak dirty, others desire a more clean approach. You should know the woman you are speaking to and know when to use slang, explicit or sexual innuendos.

CHAPTER 6: THE ART OF ROMANCE

A man is truly a man when he wins the love of a good woman, earns her respect, and keeps her trust. Until you do that, you're not a man.
(Gregory David Roberts)

Described as the feeling of excitement and mystery associated with love, romance brings passion and excitement to a relationship which would otherwise deteriorate. Romance is truly a nebulous thing. It is easily describable but not so easily definable. Women, in particular, crave romance, and being loving and affectionate.

Excitement

Raise her interest in you by making her feel warm inside with random acts of spontaneity to make her adrenaline rush. Remember a woman is still a woman. Whether she is religious, unmarried or a self-professed feminist, her desire for love, affection and appreciation does not change. A woman will always be a woman. As long as you can satisfy these needs she is more likely to try and satisfy your needs for sexual gratification.

In order to create excitement in your romantic gestures, you must be creative and make an effort. Predictability and lack of effort will not create excitement in her heart. You must put in the work.

People will forget what you said, people will forget what you did, but people will never forget how you made them feel.
(Maya Angelou)

Mystery

Romance is often associated with the feeling of mystery. Women love mysterious and spontaneity in a man. There is an old saying that "familiarity breeds contempt." Mystery intrigues women, as they project their fantasies and desires on mysterious men. Being mysterious and elusive should not be confused with deceitfulness.[94] Though they may appear to be similar, they are actually worlds apart. American author Robert Greene said in *The Art of Seduction*:

> An elusive, enigmatic aura will make people want to know more, drawing them into your circle... The moment people feel they know what to expect from you, your spell on them is broken.[95]

Tips to Become Mysterious:

- Be distant from her, from time to time.
- Have an aura about yourself.
- Do not talk a lot.
- Do not be predictable and boring
- Do not tell a woman everything about your plans, as the African proverb states.

Do not speak loudly about your plans because a roaring lion catches no prey.

---

[94] Nasheed, 2005, pp. 112-113.
[95] See Robert Greene, *The Art of Seduction.*

Love

The Oxford dictionary, defines love as "a strong feeling of affection and sexual attraction for someone." Originated from the Old English word *lufu* of German origin. The word is derived from an Indo-European root word shared by the Sanskrit word *lubhyati* (desires) and Latin *libet* (pleasing) and *libido* (desire). Love has many definitions and meanings to people. It is an ineffable matter that many have struggled to explain its nature and reality.

Love is of different types; love of God, love of family, friends, religion, spouses, children, objects etc. For the purpose of this book we are speaking about sexual love. The (sexual) love that a man has for a woman, or the (sexual) love that a woman has for a man. Sexual love is the mutually satisfying sharing of each other's experience and the experience of each other – with no built-in time requirement. Sexual love has also been described as the harmony of two souls and the contact of two bodies. Alex Comfort said:

> "Many of the people who talk loudest about love, in its conventional meaning of making someone live up to their expectations, are neurotics incapable of loving anyone except themselves."[96]

A Woman's Love

A woman's love as, African-American author Steve Harvey writes, "stands the test of time, logic, and all circumstance." A woman's love is like no other, "Nothing on this planet can compare with a woman's love — it is kind and compassionate, patient and

[96] Comfort, 1987, *More Joy of Sex* vol. 2, p. 151.

nurturing, generous and sweet and unconditional." Pure and unadulterated, a woman's love is oft-forgiving and encompassing. When a woman is in love with a man, she can even forgive acts of unfaithfulness. It is a baffling how encompassing a woman's love is. The one thing that can stop her love is when she loses trust in a man. It is not the act of infidelity which many women cannot ultimately take, it's the deceit involved. When a woman loses trust, her love will soon follow. Lou Paget wrote:

> Every woman in the world wants to know in her heart of hearts that he can and will take care of her physically and emotionally, and every woman wants to feel special and appreciated.[97]

If a woman loves a man, she will give it to him even through a hole in a door.[98]
(Moroccan proverb)

Falling in love is easy, staying in love is the hustle.
(African proverb)

Where there is love, there is no darkness.
(Burundi proverb)

If a woman doesn't love you, she calls you brother.
(Ivorian proverb)

Love has to be shown by deeds, not words.
(Swahili proverb)

[97] Paget, 2011, p. 63.
[98] Johnson Hodari, 2009, p. 56

CHAPTER 7: THE ART OF SEDUCTION

It is not enough to conquer, one must also know how to seduce.[99]
(Voltaire)

Women love being seduced. They love the way it feels. Seduction makes a woman feel desired, beautiful, and sexy at the same time. Seduction itself is more mental than it is physical; involving coquetry,[100] flirtation,[101] and other acts of persuasion. It is the process of deliberately enticing a person into sexual activity. Derived from the Latin word *seducere* meaning to 'lead astray,' the term has both positive and negative connotations. Negative connotations of seduction involves deceit and manipulation whereas positive connotations of the term is synonymous with the act of charming someone. For the purpose of this book, when seduction (also referred to as "game") is used, it refers to positive seduction.

Fame cannot teach game!

Four Types of Women in the Art of Seduction:

1. A woman who knows how to be seduced, and wants to be seduced. Enjoy her she wants you.

---

[99] Francois-Marie Arouet, commonly known as Voltaire was a French writer and philosopher from the eighteenth century.
[100] Coquetry is a flirtatious act or attitude.
[101] Flirtation is to behave in a way that shows a sexual attraction for someone but is not meant to be taken seriously.

2. A woman who knows how to be seduced, but doesn't want to be seduced. She is disinterested, wait until she is ready.
3. A woman who doesn't know how to be seduced, but wants to be seduced. Encourage her and take control.
4. A woman who doesn't know how to be seduced, and doesn't want to be seduced. Leave her, she will waste your time.

Relaxation

When seducing a woman, relaxation is crucial. Relax her mind and let her conscience run free before engaging in any physical stimulation. Women need to be mentally at ease before they can fully enjoy any physical contact as Lou Paget said:

> Unless a woman feels relaxed and comfortable, then nothing you can do will rev her engine.[102]

Tips to Help Relax a Woman:

- Do not tell her to relax in an aggressive manner.
- Create an ambivalent atmosphere with candles and soothing music.
- Listen to her. Some women find speaking as a form of therapy, so make sure you lend an ear to her.
- Do something unexpected for her that she will appreciate.

---

[102] Paget, 2010, p. 72.

- Offer her a massage or book her to have one in a spa.
- Cuddle her in your arms and stroke her body and hair. Do not be quick to touch her breasts and genitalia as this may turn her off when she is not in the mood. Take your time to make her feel comfortable and she will become aroused in her own time.

Power

Women are captivated by powerful men, whether that is physical power (strength), societal power (status), financial power (wealth), psychological power (intelligence), or emotional power (personality). He who has the power has the woman, as the Nigerian proverb says:

A woman is like a horse. He who can drive her is her master.

Depending on the type of power that the woman you are trying to seduce is desirous of, you should try and attain this power and then she is likely to be more agreeable to your seductive methods.

The Power of Money

Women desire security, especially financial security, in order to feel attracted to a man. Many women believe money can buy happiness and they will compromise love for financial stability. Financial security will help a woman feel more at ease and relaxed, which is very important if you want to seduce her.

It is also true that many women will lose their respect and desire for a man if he loses his money.

Although most women are not attracted to a man simply for his money, money can definitely help in the seduction process, as the saying goes; "There is no romance without finance."
Money most definitely helps in the seductive process as the erotologist Ibn Yahya informs:

> A man cannot gain the love a woman without money. If he tries to gain her love only through sexual union she will turn to somebody else. However, money should be combined with a man's sexual capacity.[103]

Several Yoruba proverbs also informs about the importance of money for some women:

Only money is hard to come by; a wife is not hard to come by.
(If one has money, finding a wife is a simple matter).[104]

Women care only about money.[105]
(Yoruba proverb warning against some women who are primarily motivated by money, i.e. gold-diggers.)[106]

A principle of African manliness is that wealth does not define you as a man nor should you allow it to cause your destruction in order to impress a woman.

Man makes the money, money doesn't make the man.

Do not rely on superficial material items to attract women. Material things like; money, houses, and cars,

---

103 Ibn Yaḥyā, p. 90.
104 Owomoyela, 2005, p. 287.
105 Owomoyela, 2005, p. 252.
106 Gold-digger is a woman who becomes or tries to become romantically involved with a rich man in order to get money and gifts from him.

is not a requirement to attract women, though it can definitely help. You should not rely on material items to attract women or to validate your manliness. Validation and confidence comes from within first and foremost.

Quotes and Proverbs about Money

Money can't buy love, nor save a marriage.

Money may not be able to buy her love but it will definitely make her pay attention.

You can lose a lot of money chasing women, but you will never lose women chasing money.

Yoruba proverbs:

Limit how often you take a bath; it is wealth that grooms a person.
(Wealth beautifies more efficiently than a lot of grooming.)[107]

One does not carry debt around one's neck and live like a dandy.
(One should discharge one's obligations before indulging in extravagances.[108]

One does not live fashionably on borrowed money.[109]
(One should live within their means. Do not get yourself into debt or sacrifice your principles for a woman, even though you may want to impress her.)

[107] Owomoyela, 2005, p. 280.
[108] Owomoyela, 2005, p. 42.
[109] Owomoyela, 2005, p. 43.

Mental Penetration

Stimulate her mind before you penetrate her body.

Women are highly sexual and emotional creatures. They love sex as much, if not more than men. Women want to be seduced all the time, not just when you are in the bedroom. The mistake many men make is that they neglect the importance of mental stimulation. Women crave foreplay, especially mental foreplay prior to physical foreplay. The sensual nature of a woman is stronger than a man's. For a woman, sex must include much more than physical penetration. She wants to be emotionally stimulated as much as she wants to be physically penetrated. There are many ways to mentally stimulate a woman and you should be well-versed in the multiple ways to penetrate her mind before you penetrate her body.

Never push your woman to do something sexually, instead you should lead her mentally to want it.

When your woman is emotionally satisfied, you can easily satisfy her physical needs. The more emotionally connected that you are to her, the more enjoyable physical intimacy will be. It is best to only engage in sexual activity when she is mentally stimulated, as this will help create a comfort zone in her mind where she will actively participate in lovemaking.

If you kiss her mind, her body will follow.

Sex starts in a woman's mind.

The best place to make love to a woman is in her mind.

Tips to Mentally Seduce a Woman:

- Speak with your eyes. There is a lot you can say with seductive eyes alone.
- Compliment her without too much flattery.
- Absence makes the heart grow fonder.
- Instruct do not ask. Women like a man who directs her without being overly aggressive or forceful.
- In order to mentally prepare her for sex, before you get into the bedroom, tell her how you are going to make passionate love to her. The more details you give the better. Lou Paget advises:

> In the same way that getting her in the mood requires making her feel special, turning her on physically requires giving her your full attention. If she feels that you are completely engaged in the moment, focused on her, on being with her and pleasing her, she is bound in open like a flower in the midday sun.[110]

Signs That You Have Penetrated Her Mind:

- She becomes physically aroused by your presence and hearing your voice.
- Her heart beats rapidly at the thought of you.
- She regularly looks at you with bedroom eyes.[111]
- She becomes moist by your touch.
- She regularly has erotic dreams and fantasises about you.

---

[110] Paget, 2010, p. 72.

[111] When a woman really desires a man and he has mentally penetrated her, he can see the sex in her eyes when she looks at him.

Why Do White Women Fantasise About Black Men?
The legendary tales of the sexual exploits of the African Mandingo warrior and the perception of black men having large penises has helped create sexual intrigue in the minds of many females about the joys of chocolate men. Many white women, both from Europe and the Arab world, fantasise about black men which is why many European and Arab men have feared the sexual prowess of the unbridled African man sleeping with their women. Unfortunately some black men take advantage of this mental power that they hold and mistreat the women who passionately desire them. The reasons why many of these women fantasise about black men are as follows:

- They want something different and exciting.
- The desirability of the forbidden fruit.
- Perception of a large penis.
- Perception of black men being passionate lovers.
- The belief in the high virility of black men. Male stamina is crucial in women being able to reach higher states of sexual pleasure and orgasm more.
- Feel more desired by black men who tend to desire full-figured and curvaceous women as opposed to white men who tend to desire very slim women.

CHAPTER 8: THE ART OF PHYSICAL FOREPLAY

A kiss is an upper persuasion to a lower invasion.

Physical foreplay includes all physical sexual acts except for actual penetration. Although foreplay can be tedious at times as you just want to release, you should remember why you are doing it. It is to please your lady. This will make intercourse more pleasurable for the both of you. The three most essential components of physical foreplay are; kissing, fondling and embrace.

Kissing

There is nothing more arousing to women than the sensuous power of a kiss. Whether that kiss is wet, cool, brief, or lingering, alone it can have the power to bring a woman to her knees. The power of an intense kiss is mesmerising for women.[112]

If you kiss a woman well, and kiss her the way she wants to be kissed, she will be ready to please you. How you kiss her and how she likes to be kissed is also very important, but more important is to kiss her with feeling and intimacy.[113]

Lip and tongue kisses add immensely to intercourse in all face-to-face lovemaking positions. A deep tongue kiss can even be a form of penetration.

---

[112] Paget, 2010, p. 74.
[113] Paget, 2010, p. 75.

Some women can experience an orgasm by kissing alone.

Intense kisses are the most pleasurable to many women. Another pleasure is to make her a carpet of flowers, by covering every inch of her body with small, soft, close kisses. If you haven't at least kissed her mouth, shoulders, neck, breasts, arms, head, navel, earlobes and genitals, you haven't really kissed her.[114] A good kiss should leave her breathless and yearning for more. Groaning, sighs, gasping for air and her moistness are indicates that she is really enjoying your lips. Several erotologists advised couples to master the art of kissing to heighten their sexual play.

Al-Ṣuyuṭī advised:

> Do not forget to practise kissing and cuddling, and the interlocking of leg with leg, and to suck with delicate lips; at what time the mount now bites with passion and rapturous kisses, and then pats and taps with his sword-like weapon, which anon he draws forth, but only again to thrust into the expectant sheath seeking out all the nooks and crannies, and holes and corners, whilst not losing sight of the walls of the roof![115]

Muhammad al-Nafzawī said:

> The kiss is assumed to be an integral part of coition. The best kiss is the one impressed on humid lips combined

[114] Comfort, 1993, p. 129.
[115] Al-Ṣuyuṭī, 1987, p. 8.

> with the suction of the lips and tongue, which latter particularly provokes the flow of sweet and fresh saliva. It is for the man to bring this about by slightly and softly nibbling his partner's tongue, when her saliva will flow sweet and exquisite, more pleasant than refined honey, and which will not mix with the saliva of her mouth. This manoeuvre will give the man a trembling sensation, which will run all through his body, and is more intoxicating than wine drinking to excess.[116]

Every woman wants a man who can ruin her lipstick and not her mascara.

Fondling

Take the time to touch your woman's body, and not just between her legs. Explore her erogenous zones like her collar bone, the nape of her neck, her lower back, inside her knees, and her toes before you go to work on her private area.

Ibn Nasir al-Katib said:

> To excite a woman sexually, a man should rub her nipples, this way brings about a wonderful effect![117]

[116] Sheikh Nefzaoui (Muhammad al-Nafzawi) translated by Richard Burton, *The Perfumed Garden*, pp.68-69.
[117] Ibn Nasir al-Katib, 1977, p. 322.

Muhammad al-Nafzāwī said:

> When you feel the desire for intimacy, you will both find it more agreeable to perfume yourselves first. Engage in foreplay with your wife in bed, caress her and kiss her and lick her all over, on her front and her back, until you see desire quicken in her eyes. Then position yourself between her legs, insert your penis into her vagina – and do it. Foreplay beforehand will make it much more enjoyable for the two of you [as well as being gentler on your stomach].[118]

Embrace

Embrace is part of the art of sexual love which the author of *Kama Sutra* explains its various types:

> Now the embrace which indicates the mutual love of a man and woman who have come together is of four kinds:
>
> Touching
> Rubbing
> Piercing
> Pressing
>
> The action in each case is denoted by the meaning of the word which stands for it. When a man under some pretext or other goes in front or alongside of a woman and touches her body with his own, it is called the 'touching embrace.'
>
> When a woman in a lonely place bends down, as if to pick up

[118] Al-Nafzāwī, 1999, p. 34.

> something, and pierces, as it were, a man sitting or standing, with her breasts, and the man in return takes hold of them, it is called a 'piercing embrace.'
>
> The above two kinds of embrace take place only between persons who do not, as yet, speak freely with each other.
>
> When two lovers are walking slowly together, either in the dark, or in a place of public resort, or in a lonely place, and rub their bodies against each other, it is called a 'rubbing embrace.'
>
> When on the above occasion one of them presses the others body forcibly against a wall or pillar, it is called a 'pressing embrace.'
>
> These two last embraces are peculiar to those who know the intentions of each other.[119]

Ibn Falita said:

> Women like to be embraced strongly but painfully, especially when they are about to achieve an orgasm or when the man is about to achieve an orgasm.[120]

[119] See *Kama Sutra* translated by Richard Burton.
[120] Ibn Falita, 1977, p. 82.

CHAPTER 9: THE ART OF TOUCHING

Touch her, tease her, feel her, and caress her.

Most women loved to be tenderly touched. Genital touching with a combination of hand and finger stimulation can be as intimate as actual penetrative intercourse.

Manual Stimulation

Manual stimulation also known as manual play and masturbation, refers to hand and finger stimulation of the erogenous zones, particularly the genitalia. The manual stimulation that is praiseworthy in traditional African and Arab thought is mutual stimulation in which a man stimulates a woman and a woman stimulates a man. A man should not self-service himself, nor should a woman self-service herself. They should service each other for mutual pleasure.

The ability to arouse a woman to the heights of erotic pleasure with your hands and fingers is essential to lovemaking. A man who can manually stimulate his woman really skilfully can give her a truly exhilarating orgasmic experience.

Indian erotologist Kalyana Malla said:

> A woman is [like] a delicious instrument, when artfully played upon,

> she is capable of producing the most exquisite harmony.[121]

Tips for Manual Stimulation:

- Tenderness is key. Women respond better to very light than to very hard stimulation – just brushing her vagina with your fingertips will usually do more for her than a whole-hand grab.
- Use lubrication when stimulating her genitalia.
- Trim your fingernails to avoid discomfort.
- Ensure that your hands are clean.

Fingering Techniques

Fingering is the use of the finger to stimulate the vagina. It is very effective in bringing a woman to arousal and climax. Some women find it easier to experience an orgasm when stimulated with the fingers than through oral stimulation or actual penetration.

Clinical sexologist Ian Kerner and Lou Paget makes mention of dozens of fingering techniques to satisfy a woman in their books, *She Comes First: The Thinking Man's Guide to Pleasuring a Woman* and *How to Give Her Absolute Pleasure.* Some of these techniques are mentioned below.

Come-Hither Technique

- Start with a straight index finger and then curl it in a "come-hither" gesture.

---

[121] See *Ananga Ranga* translated by Richard Burton.

- Gently graze her vaginal ceiling with your fingertip. As you do so, your finger will pass over the clitoral cluster, an area of sensitive spongy tissue that surrounds the urethra and swells against the vaginal ceiling when aroused. At this point in the process of arousal, her clitoral cluster should be fairly easy to find, as it is likely engorged with the inflow of blood. Your fingertip should end its journey in the spongy tissue where her vaginal ceiling intersects with her vaginal entrance. In addition, press lightly against her pubic bone with your fingertip.

Clitoral-Cluster Squeeze Technique

- Press the length of your finger against her vaginal ceiling – hold the position and apply pressure against the area. Don't be shy about pressing up into her vaginal ceiling. The clitoral cluster is less sensitive than the clitoral head, and responds well to firm, persistent pressure.

- As you press your finger into her vaginal ceiling, use your free hand to press down from above on her pubic mound. The pressure from above compliments the pressure from below and heightens the sensitivity of the region to your touch.

Perineal Pinch Technique

- Use your index finger to stroke the vaginal floor. This will excite her perineal tissue (the sensitive erectile tissue that lines the expanse of skin between her vagina and anus).

- When stimulating her perineal tissue from the inside with your index finger, use your thumb to press her perineum from the outside. In this position, you are literally pinching her perineum from both sides.

Double Finger Technique

- Insert your index and middle finger inside her vaginal canal (palm up) and maintain a still position. Take a moment to feel her pelvic muscles contract against the sides of your fingers; notice the further tightening of her vaginal entrance (the clitoral cuff) around your fingers.

- Use both fingers, firmly locked together, to graze the ceiling, floor and walls of her vagina with come-hither gestures. When grazing her vaginal ceiling feel your fingertips pass over the spongy tissue of the clitoral cluster.

- Flatten your fingers and press them into her vaginal ceiling. Push up against the spongy tissue. Apply firm pressure. With your other hand, press down against her pubic mound.[122]

Three Fold Technique

- Use your three fingers (index, middle and 'ring' finger) held together to curve the inner and

---

[122] Kerner, 2010, pp. 134-142.

outer lips of her vagina. Keep your index finger and ring finger on the outer edges of her labia while your middle finger is positioned on top of the entire clitoral clitoral ridge and bud.

- Maintain a slow up-and-down or circular motion. Then subtly slip the middle finger inside the vagina. Finally, with your index and middle fingers together, do a short range of motion over the clitoral ridge, moving from front to back, with a gentle squeeze, or a pulse up and down.[123]

Massage Techniques

In his ground-breaking book, *A Celebration of Sex: A Guide to Enjoying God's Gift of Sexual Intimacy*, licensed psychologist and Christian sex therapist Dr. Douglas Rosenau identified five basic massage techniques for couples to enhance their lovemaking experience.

1. Stroking

The stroking technique is essentially long gentle movements with your hands along a portion of the body. Keep your fingers together, thumbs parallel and palms in full contact with the body part you are massaging. Stroking is a common massage technique and one which is pleasurable on most areas of the body.

---

[123] Paget, 2011, pp. 119-120.

2. Kneading

Kneading is a technique that can be used on large fleshy areas of the body like the soft tissue of the lower back and the buttocks, as well as smaller fleshy areas like the shoulders, thighs and calves. Kneading relaxes the muscles as it stimulates blood circulation. In order to massage the deeper muscles, firm pressure should be applied, to sensuously stimulate the skin, light pressure should be applied.

3. Knuckling

The knuckling technique consists of applying small circular strokes to create a pleasant rippling effect. The knuckling technique is particularly effective on the back, shoulders and chest. It can also be enjoyed on the palms of the hands or soles of the feet.

4, Pummelling

The important part of this technique, whether you are using a loose fist or relaxed hand, is to use bouncy motions and not strike the flesh. Pull your hand away as soon as it touches the skin so there is no bruising pressure. It helps to keep the wrists loose and hands and fingers relaxed so you can hear them slapping together, and the motion should be brisk as you rapidly stimulate. Sometimes pummelling might be better reserved for the end of the massage, though it can be relaxing if done more gently. It is great for fleshy areas like the back or thighs, where there are heavier muscles.

5. Passive Touching

You don't always have to be actively stroking or massaging a body area. Simply placing a hand on a spot as the partner's body feels the warmth or pressure (if applied) really feels good as tissue is stimulated by the passive touch. Passive touch also includes pulling or rotating a part of the body to loosen up and exercise joints without actively stroking.

CHAPTER 10: THE ART OF LOVEMAKING

Men who say women belong in the kitchen, obviously do not know what to do with them in the bedroom.

Lovemaking is sexual play and sexual activity between lovers, especially including sexual intercourse. The three main sexual activities of lovemaking are cunnilingus, fellatio and sexual intercourse. Cunnilingus is oral stimulation of the female genitalia. Fellatio, commonly referred to as "getting head," is oral stimulation of the male penis.

Cunnilingus

There is an art to oral play. It involves a combination of kissing, biting, licking and sucking her private area. You should take your time whilst exploring her vagina. Slow, rhythmic thrusts with your tongue will increase her sexual pleasure.

In many ways the tongue is better than the penis in the art of lovemaking. The more subtle, rhythmic movements of the tongue are more suited to the gradual female sexual arousal process than the harder penetrative thrusting of the penis. When using the tongue, a man does not have to worry about growing fatigued, has no time constraints, and the tongue is effective when hard or soft. Under direct control, the tongue can be manipulated with expert precision to please his lady.[124]

Men who are not well versed in the art of cunnilingus should try to master some of the oral techniques to help their lady seek ultimate pleasure. Giving expert cunnilingus requires learning appropriate techniques and then applying them consistently over time in a focused, patient, and loving manner. Most importantly, it requires respecting, sharing and participating wholly in the erotic intimacy of the moment. Every woman loves to have her pussy sucked, provided that it is done the correct way.

To be truly effective in cunnilingus it is important for the man to psychologically prepare his woman for the act and make her feel at ease and assured of her sexuality. He can obtain this by smiling at her whilst performing oral sex, complimenting her and telling her how sweet she tastes. These minute but crucial acts will not only enable her to relax better but it will also make it easier for her to attain an orgasm.[125] Ian Kerner lists the following guidance for cunnilinguists:

- Respect the female process of arousal
- Postpone self-gratification in the pursuit of mutual pleasure
- Know and appreciate the clitoris in all its manifold aspects
- Stimulate the clitoral appropriately through the entire process of sexual response.

---

[124] Kerner, 2010, p. 29-30.
[125] Kerner, 2010, p. 31.

- Dispense with the conventional wisdom that exalts genital penetration as the apogee of sexual pleasure.
- Purge yourself of stereotypes, clichés, and prejudices.
- Be patient, respectful, sensitive, and tender.
- Take an approach that is pleasure-orientated, not goal orientated.
- Approach each act as a unique process of giving and receiving, knowing and learning.
- Give of yourself seriously, generously, and wholeheartedly.[126]

It is important to remember that you should always give the impression that "going down on her" is enjoyable for you and it turns you on just as much as much as it turns her on. This will help her relax and heighten her arousal. You should take your time and savour the moment, a master cunnilinguist is not selfish with his time. You should also give the impression that you enjoy her smell and taste as many women are insecure about this. [127]

Every woman smells and tastes different. Some are sweeter than others, some are a bit more pungent, whilst others are more neutral and nondescript. Sometimes the differences are subtle, other times they are stark. Nor will the same woman consistently smell or taste the same. Lots of factors can affect vaginal smell and taste, including diet, vitamin deficiencies, medication, menstruation cycle, infection, hydration, alcohol, tobacco and unprotected sex because sperm is highly alkaline and raises the pH level of the vaginal

---

[126] Kerner, 2010, pp. 80-81.
[127] Kerner, 2010, pp. 81-82.

ecosystem. A woman with an odious vaginal smell, in some sense, may be indicative of promiscuity, which is probably why ancient erotologists described licentious women as having foul-smelling vaginas.[128]

Effective Positions to Perform Cunnilingus;

- The Straight On
- T-Cross
- Legs Together
- Her Leg Over His Shoulder
- Side by Side
- 69 Position
- Downward Dog
- Loving the Prize
- Hovering Butterfly
- The Arch
- Rear Approach
- Chair Therapy
- Stand and Deliver

Fellatio

Women who have really learned to enjoy sex are usually fascinated by their partner's penis, as men are by women's breasts, shape, odor and feel, and learn to play with it fully and skilfully. Good hand and mouth work [will] practically [make] a good partner.
(Alex Comfort)[129]

There is nothing like receiving fellatio from a beautiful woman. It is a selfless act done by a woman where she

[128] Kerner, 2010, pp. 69-70.
[129] Comfort, 1993, p. 34.

defers her own sexual gratification to give you sexual pleasure. When a woman performs oral sex it is the ultimate act of sexual submission that a woman can do. Many women are unaware of the high regard men have for a woman who performs oral sex on him, especially those who are skilful at performing the act.

Fellatio is part of the lovemaking experience and a woman who gives you good oral sex is likely to increase your desire to want to please her. However not all women have the natural skillset to perform oral sex well. Many require instruction and encouragement to master the art.

Women love the penis as much as men love the vagina. Many women will deny their love of performing fellatio out of fear of being perceived as filthy or immoral. You need to earn her trust before she will give you the "special attention" that most men crave.

Tips to Help Her Master the Art of Fellatio

- Let her know what you like in a calm manner.
- Do not shout or say anything disrespectful.
- Compliment her and tell her how much you are enjoying the experience.
- Make erotic noises when she is doing a good job so that it will encourage her to continue.

Lovemaking Techniques

It's the first time together and I'm feeling kind of horny.
Conventional methods of making love kind of bore me.
(James Todd Smith aka "LL Cool J")

There are many ways to make love, al-Nafzawi advises, "You must thus enjoy a woman in whatever position you please [apart from the anus],[130] as all are known to be permissible." The standard man-on-top missionary position is the not always the most pleasurable for adult play. Thus, erotologists detailed a number of lovemaking positions and techniques in their works to help spice up the sexual relationships of their readers.

Lovemaking Technique Tips

Al-Nafzawi makes mention of the following lovemaking techniques:

- Let your wife lie upon her back and raise her thighs, take up a squatting position, between them and penetrate her. This is a suitable position for the larger penis.

- The woman lies upon her back and lifts her knees up to either side of her head, so that her buttocks are raised and her vulva protrudes; then penetrate her. This position is suitable for the smaller penis.

- Have the woman lie upon her back then position yourself between her thighs, place one of her legs over your shoulder, the other under your arm and penetrate her.

- Let the woman lie upon her back and place her legs upon your arm and penetrate her.

[130] Anal sex also known as sodomy, is not a lovemaking act befitting of a male. Why would you want to enter the anus when you have the vagina?!

- Let the woman lie upon her back and place her legs upon your shoulder; then enter her.

- While both of you lie on your side, part the woman's legs and penetrate her.

- The woman gets down on her elbows and knees and you penetrate her from behind [in her vagina].

- Have your wife lie on her side and kneel between her thighs, place her top leg on your shoulder and the other between your thighs. She stays lying on her side as you penetrate her, at the same time hugging her to your breast and caressing her.

- Let the woman lie with her legs folded under her and place your knees one on either side of her so that her legs are between your thighs; then penetrate her.

- Have her lie on a low divan or chair, either face down with her knees on the ground or with her back on the sear, her feet on the ground and her buttocks resting on the angle of the chair, then penetrate her.

- With both hands, the woman holds onto a suitably low branch of a tree. You place her legs around your waist and have her keep them there. Penetrate her while you are also holding onto the branch and the more you thrust, the more she will rock to and fro.

- Have her lie down and place a cushion or pillow under her buttocks. Spread her thighs wide and, placing the soles of her feet together, position yourself between her knees and penetrate her.[131]

Make-Up Sex is The Best Sex

Make-up sex is wild and extremely gratifying sex that couples have after an intense fight or argument. Engaging in a sexual reconciliation after a long, gut-wrenching argument makes the entire acrimonious experience worthwhile.

The great excitement generated by make-up sex can be explained due to the transfer of the high arousal state associated with the fight to a high arousal state during the make-up sex. Make-up sex is also particularly exhilarating because it ensues a pleasant reconciliation after an unpleasant disagreement.[132]

It is normal to have an argument with your woman or get into some form of conflict. However, you should try and not get into regular arguments with her as she will lose her respect for you. Stay calm and let her say what she has to say by venting her anger. Getting things off her chest is therapeutic for many women and will help her relax. After she has let off some steam, then you may proceed to passionately penetrate her.

---

[131] Al-Nafzawi, 1999, pp. 35-36.
[132] Ben-Zeév, Aaron, "Why Make-Up Sex And Breakup Sex Are So Good."

Make-Up Sex Positions:

- **Up Against The Wall Position** – Pin her against the wall and insert your penis into her vagina in a controlled aggressive but not forceful manner. Many women love this approach but like with all things you have to know what she desires.

  Put her hands above her head and raise one of her thighs as you thrust your penis into her vagina with gusto. It is important to maintain a calm composure to extend this lovemaking experience as it is very pleasurable and can cause you to ejaculate very quickly.

  The up against the wall position provides superb clitoral stimulation when done properly. The woman should stand a foot away from the wall, with her back leaning against it. You should stand in close proximity to her, with your legs straddled and knees slightly bent.

  This position requires considerable amount of physical strength, so you should not over exert yourself with the initial thrusting. Stay calm and composed to prolong the sexual experience for both you and your lady.

  Although rough and slightly aggressive, this sexual position should be controlled, but most importantly with your lady's consent.

- **Rear Entry Position** - The classic vaginal rear entry ('doggy-style') position is a very gratifying lovemaking position for men and women. The lack of face-to-faceness of this position is more than compensated for by the extra depth and buttock stimulation, and hand access to her breasts and clitoris.

  The rear entry position is especially enjoyable for men as it gives him a sense of power and control of the sexual activity. The rear entry position is particularly enjoyable for men with women who have large and prominent buttocks.

  As any man who has enjoyed the pleasures of a woman with large buttocks knows, there is nothing like the rear-entry position. But your penis must be long enough to fully penetrate her vagina from behind. If you are not well-endowed you should try an alternative position, like the woman-on-top position to allow penetration to the extra sensitive vaginal walls.

  Women also enjoy this position as it allows the deepest penetration possible of the vagina, and allows the penis to directly stimulate the G-spot, thus increasing her sexual pleasure. For increased and deeper penetration, the woman should lower her face as low as possible, whilst keeping her buttocks as high as possible.

As men tend to ejaculate very quickly in this position, you can try shallow thrusts to maximise your pleasure because the opening and first third of the vagina is more sensitive than the rest of her genitalia.

Which Women are the Best at Sexual Intercourse?

Al-Suyuti narrated that when Harith, a renowned physician of the Arabs, was asked by [the Persian Emperor] Chosroes I,

> "Which women are the best [in beauty and sexual intercourse]?" Harith answered,
>
> "A woman who possesses the form of the women of Madinah [are the best]. She is above average height, has a large forehead, firm nostrils, pale white skin and cheeks of perfect form. Her overaching eyelashes are ornamented and meet together across a nose of pride like lovers stealing a kiss. She has well-formed, pearly-white teeth flashing with smiles. Her posterior is large and rotund, her shoulders broad and well-thrown back; her whole body poised upon tiny feet which in suppleness and softness of allurement resemble the grace and beauties of the houris of Paradise.
>
> And as for the best from the other women; there are the women of the Greeks, who have the cleanest vulvas, broadest buttocks, are well-adapted to a [graceful] sitting posture and enjoy

intercourse. As for the women of Andalusia [modern day Spain]; they have the most beautiful faces and the sweetest smell. The women of India, Sindh and Sicily [in Italy] are the most reprehensive in their conditions, the ugliest features, the dirtiest vulvas and the most unintelligent. The daughters of Zanzibar [in Tanzania] and Abyssinia [modern day Ethiopia] are by nature the most sweet-smelling and the most obedient of women. As for the women of Baghdad and Babylonia [in Iraq], they are the most voluptuousness in the act of making love. As for the women of Syria; they are the most unkind towards men. Bedouin and Persian women are the most charming in respect of their secret conditions, and their children are the most intelligent; for eloquence they are unrivalled, and in terms of sociability, they outshine all other women! Their faithfulness is well known.

Kenyan and Nubian women [i.e. northern Sudan] have the most feverous vulvas, the largest buttocks, the softest bodies and the most passionate of women for sexual intercourse. As for Turkish women, they have the uncleanest private parts, are the most fertile and have the worst tempers. They are the most rancorous in disposition and the least gifted with brains.

> The women of Bosra [in Syria] are the most intense lovers of men. The women of Aleppo are very powerful in body structure and between their legs, they are the most solidly-constructed. The women of Egypt are the most seductive in speech, refined in character, and as for the art of licentiousness, they exceed in it which many stories document. The women in Upper Egypt are the most pleasurable to lie with and to mount. Of all the women in the world, it is reported that the beautiful daughters [i.e. women] of Lower Egypt possess the greatest vulvas and the peasant women that reside in the borders of the Nile are the strongest in desire for a large-sized penis."[133]

The aforementioned narration is not representative of all erotologists as the area is a subjective matter.

When the lights go out, it's all one colour.

No woman is inherently better than another because of her colour or ethnicity. What distinguishes the pleasurability of one woman from another lies in her ability to arouse her man's desire, the feeling he has in his heart for her, and her lovemaking abilities. A combination of these factors will result in an exhilarating and pleasurable sexual experience that they both will never forget.

---

[133] Al-Ḥasanī, 2011, pp. 132-133, Al-Suyuti, 1987, pp. 67-72.

CHAPTER 11: THE ART OF SATISFACTION

The truth is. Most women do not have satisfying sex lives...better sex is about one thing: better orgasm.
(Nicole Daedone)

Satisfaction is the fulfilment of a need, want or desire. Most erotologists placed the onus of pleasuring a woman on the man. However, true satisfaction requires effort from both the man and the woman. Satisfaction is more pleasurable when the two are both active participants. The real pleasure is felt when the lover sees that their beloved is also satisfied as Alex Comfort said:

Real lovers get a reward not only from their own satisfactions but from seeing the other respond and become satisfied.[134]

Female Satisfaction

Women are pleasured treasures.

Erotologist Kalyana Malla said:

> Satisfaction and enjoyment comes for a man with possession of a beautiful woman. Men marry because of the peaceful gathering, love, and comfort and they often get nice and attractive women. But the men do not give the women full satisfaction. The reason is due to the ignorance of the writings of

[134] Comfort, 1993, p. 15.

> the *Art of Love* and the disdain of the different types of women. These men view women only from the perspective of an animal. They are foolish and spiritless.[135]

Before a man can satisfy a woman he needs to understand her. Each woman has her own way in which she wants to be satisfied. The man needs to be confident in his ability to satisfy her needs. Very often men who suffer from performance anxiety lack self-confidence and fail miserably in satisfying their lady's desires.

A woman is a necessity to a man's life and not an accessory.

Ibn Falita said:

> [Women like a man] who is capable of delaying ejaculation long enough for her to achieve sexual climax.[136]

Al-Suyuti said:

> The most beloved man to women is the one who has the greatest sexual endurance.[137]

Women probably differ sexually more than men. Never assume that you don't need to relearn for each person.
(Alex Comfort)[138]

---

[135] See *Ananga Ranga* translated by Richard Burton.
[136] Ibn Falita, 1977, p. 29.
[137] Al-Suyuti, 2011, vol. 1, p. 236.
[138] Comfort, 1993, p. 44.

Four Types of Women in the Bedroom

- **Expert** – Master of the art of lovemaking. An expert is a woman who takes pleasure in satisfying her lover and can teach you some things about the art of lovemaking.

- **Adventurous** – Willing to try out new methods or experiences. She is full of excitement and enthusiasm. She requires instruction and for you to take charge.

- **Insecure** – A timid woman who lacks sexual confidence. Sex with an insecure woman can be extremely uncomfortable and unsatisfying. She requires reassurance and patience.

- **Frigid** – Frigid women are unresponsive in the bedroom and will just lay there like a living corpse. If your woman is disinterested, you should leave her, and not force or threaten her to perform any sexual act.

A woman can be a combination of the aforementioned types depending on her mood. Alternatively, a woman can be frigid with one male and adventurous with another because the latter has awoken her sexual desire.

Every woman is a [sexual] freak but not every man can bring that freak out of her.[139]

[139] A sexual freak is a person who sexually adventurous individual. It is also used to refer to a nymphomaniac, a woman with an extremely high sex drive.

The Emotional Nature of Women

Women are emotional by nature, whereas men are more rational by nature. The emotional nature of women is not a deficiency in their disposition. It is how they were created. Many men struggle with the emotional aspect of women and incorrectly think that they are "crazy" due to their different composition.

One of the most troubling matters which men have issues with in regards to women, is their tendency to nag, complain and blame others without taking responsibility. Ignore this and do not take it personally. Women often do not take accountability for their actions due to their emotional nature. They will personalise issues if you speak about matters pertaining to women and take it as a personal attack. If you as a man were to criticise her for something she has done wrong, her first response is likely to try and deflect the criticism by mentioning something which you have done wrong or blame you. This trait is common amongst many women and as a man you have to know how to deal with this by being silent and patient. Eventually she will calm down and you can proceed to enjoy her again.

A passionate woman is worth the chaos.

Women who Withhold Sex

Erotologists warned men about women who withhold sex from their husbands out of spitefulness. The power of sex is the strongest trump card that a woman has over men and some women will intentionally use sex as a weapon against their husbands in order to control and manipulate them. Such women are extremely selfish.

If a woman is withholding sex from her man he should replace her with a woman who would not do such a despicable thing.

If you as a man are fulfilling your marital duties to her and are treating her with kindness, but she is adamant in punishing you by withholding sexual gratification out of spitefulness, you need to seriously think about replacing her.

According to Professor Olugboyega Alaba, in his article, *Understanding Sexuality in the Yoruba Culture,* when a married woman denies her husband intimacy, elders will try and reconcile the issue by reminding her of her marital duties.[140] Sexual intimacy amongst the Yoruba, like many of the African and Arab nations is an essential part of a marital relationship.

A Woman's Tricks

Many erotologists spent a great deal of time discussing female deceptiveness. It is a characteristic which is inherent in some women who are selfish and vindictive. Erotologists warned men not to be deceived by a woman's attractiveness as some of the greatest liars are the most beautiful and innocent looking women. Deceitful women are very smart and cunning when they want to me. Some of these women can scheme for years to get what they want from a man.

Whilst men may play the game, women know the score.

In a [Western] society where women are not socialised to be accountable for their actions, you must be very cautious with the woman you choose to sleep

[140] Alaba, 2004, pp. 8-9.

with. Many men assume that a woman is pure of heart just because she is beautiful or because he loves her. Al-Nafzawi said that a woman's tricks are more powerful than the devil's!

A woman who has six lovers; the six lovers never know about one another.
(Yoruba proverb meaning women are past mistresses of deceit).[141]

The other type of woman which erotologists warned men about was the adulterous woman. A man should not be a cuckold and tolerate such acts of unfaithfulness. In such situations, the man should not hit the woman or force himself upon her. Rather he should let her go.

If one catches a penis in a woman's vagina, she will argue that it is only a corncob.
(Yoruba proverb meaning that a deceitful woman will protest her innocence even when caught in the act).[142]

The other dangerous type of woman you should be wary of is the lying, deceitful woman who falsely accuses men of mistreatment, or even rape. We ask God to protect us from such women.

Time is valuable, do not waste your time on a woman who is not going to bring you a good return.

Women are caps; they never accompany the hunter into the dense forest.
(Yoruba proverb meaning that some women do not stick around when the going gets tough).[143]

---

[141] Owomoyela, 2005, p. 250.
[142] Owomoyela, 2005, p. 242.
[143] Owomoyela, 2005, p. 305.

Hell has no fury like a woman scorned.
(English proverb meaning that there is nothing as unpleasant as a woman who has been offended or whose love has not been returned. It is a warning to men, informing them that when a woman is angry, she can do the most vindictive and spiteful of things to him).

Four Types Of Women, Men Should Avoid:

- **Prostitute** is a woman who engages in sexual activity for monetary payment.
- **Harlot** is a promiscuous woman who engages in casual sexual relations with a number of men. Also known as a whore.
- **Cock tease** is a woman who acts in a sexual manner to seduce a man without actually fulfilling the expected sexual activity.
- **Attention whore** is a woman who regularly solicits attention from men through unnecessary or overbearing means.

You can't make a hoe a housewife.[144]
(African-American saying)

Four Sexual Activities Some Men Desire But Are Disrespectful Towards Women

- **"Running trains"** is where a number of men engage in sexual intercourse with a single woman willingly, in the same period, one after the other. The men take turns to penetrate the woman where she also may perform sexual

[144] A hoe is a slang term for a whore.

favours on each of them. This sexual act is also referred to as a "train-ram" or a "gangbang."

- **"Tag-team"** is where two men have sexual intercourse with one woman, one after the other in one sexual session. This sexual act is also referred to as "double-team."
- **"Threesome"** is a sexual act involving three people, sometimes referred to as a *menage a trois*. A threesome is where a man engages in sexual relations with two women simultaneously, or two men having sexual relations with one woman at the same time.
- **"Orgy"** is a sexual party involving numerous people partaking in numerous sexual acts at the same sexual session. An orgy is also referred to as "group sex," and may involve a number of men and women.

Mub'abbirah, The Wise Woman

Muhammad al- Nafzāwī narrated:

> Mub'abbirah, reckoned to be the most worldly-wise woman of her day, was once asked,
>
> "Where is a woman's reason located?"
>
> "Between her legs."
>
> "And her pleasure?"
>
> "In the same place."
>
> "And her love or loathing for a man?"
>
> "Inside her vagina. If a woman loves a man, she will give him her vagina unreservedly but if she dislikes him, she will deny him. A woman will do all that she can for the man she loves and try to satisfy him in every possible way, no matter how trivial. She accepts him as he is, even if he is penniless. But if a woman dislikes a man, she will keep him at a distance, no matter how rich he would make her."

"And where is the place of a woman's perception, her passion and discernment?"

"In her eye, her heart and her vagina."

"Would you explain that?"

"Perception resides in the eye, passion in the heart and discernment, or taste, in the vagina. If a woman's eye spots a handsome man and is pleased by what it sees then affection and desire will penetrate her heart and passion, too, may find dwelling there. The woman tracks the man of her desire and sets traps for him. If she succeeds and makes sexual contact, her vagina tastes him and her taste discerns his sweetness or his bile. A woman's discernment is in her vagina and there, by taste, she knows the good man from the bad."

Then she was asked,

"What kinds of penis do women like most? What kind of woman enjoys frequent lovemaking? What kind of woman prefers infrequent lovemaking? What kind of man, is most attractive to women and what kind is least attractive?"

"Women differ in respect of their vaginas, their lovemaking and what they find attractive and unattractive to men. As women differ in physical stature so, likewise, do they differ in character. Men, too, differ in respect of their penises, their lovemaking and what they find attractive and unattractive in women.

The woman whose vagina is shallow enjoys the short, wide-calibre penis that fills her without going too far. She will find the longer penis uncomfortable. However, a woman with a deep vagina enjoys the attentions of a well-endowed man, of the soft that will fill her completely. She will have no inclination towards the short, narrow penis, which will not excite her sexually.

The temperaments of women are: bilious, melancholic, phlegmatic, sanguine or a combination of these. Women of the two former temperaments do not enjoy frequent lovemaking and are compatible only with men having the same temperament. Women of the latter two temperaments enjoy frequent and regular intercourse. If such a woman becomes aroused, she is insatiable! However, only a man of the same temperament will be compatible with her. If a man and woman of opposing temperaments marry, they will both be miserable and unhappy. Women of mixed temperament display characteristics of both types.

The women of short stature enjoy regular and frequent intercourse – more frequently, at any rate, than a tall woman. She is compatible with the well-endowed man, the like of whom will gladden her bed and lighten her life.

Men are similar to women in respect of frequency of intercourse and with regard to temperament. However, women appear to be more enamoured with a man's penis than men are with a woman's vulva."

She was then asked to say something about the worst sorts of women,

"The worst sort of woman is one who would, for example, use her own money to buy dinner then object if anyone else ate. There is the type who digs up and discloses matters you would rather remained private. There is the envious woman or the loud, shrill woman who raises her voice above her husband's, the gossip and malicious woman, the sullen, scowling woman, the hussy who makes a show of her beauty and charms and the trollop who is never at home. This woman who is often seen laughing or standing at folk's door is a slut. There is the busy-body and the nag, the scheming or spiteful woman and the light-fingered woman who pilfers her husband's money and her friends' belongings.

There is the slovenly, the frivolous and the ungrateful woman, the woman who avoids the marital bed or who initiates lovemaking with her husband and then puts him off, of the two-faced, lying, disloyal and deceitful woman. There is the troublemaker and the shrew, or the dreary woman who thinks the worst of others, the loud-mouthed and pretentious woman and the dull, simple-minded woman.

Take it from me – these are the worst sorts of women."[145]

Sexual Satisfaction Quotes and Proverbs

A man who knows how to satisfy his woman does not fear her being unfaithful.

As a man you should take pride in ensuring that you have satisfied your woman's desires.

There is nothing like satisfying your lady. It will bring you great joy and added pleasure. When you satisfy her, she will satisfy you.

A fresh vagina wakes up a weak penis.
(Ghanian proverb)[146]

A woman never forgets a man that can satisfy her physical and mental desires.

We live in strange times, where many men are content with titillation without penetration, and lusting without loving.[147]

[145] al-Nafzawī, 1999, pp. 63-65.
[146] Johnson, Hodari, 2009, p. 57
[147] Meaning that sexually frustrated men are content with voyeurism like watching pornography, lusts after women on the internet sexually harasses women in public and visits private strip-clubs instead of engaging with sexual intercourse with a woman.

The ideal husband that women desire from a man in the bedroom is a man who is; a wonderful kisser, passionate lover and can repeatedly bring her to orgasm, through intercourse and oral stimulation.

Tease her before you please her.

It is better to please than be pleased.

Real pleasure lies in mutual pleasure.

Any man can make a woman sweat, but only a real man can keep her wet.

Loyalty and orgasms, that's all she wants

People who say sex is not important in life are clearly not having good sex.

Tips to Satisfy Her:

- **Ask her** how she likes to be satisfied, you may not know unless you ask.
- **Give her multiple orgasms** and she will never forget you.
- **Maintain your attractiveness** (i.e. physique, grooming, status, wealth, and intelligence)
- **Take your time.** There is no need to rush.
- **Every beauty needs a beast.** Be sexually aggressive when the time requires.

- **Kiss her** – Do not forget to continue to kiss her once intercourse has started as kissing will make the sexual experience feel more intimate.

- **Remember the neck.** The neck is extremely sensitive to touch. Do not forget to gently lick, nibble and kiss her neck. You can also breathe and suck on her neck for added sensation.

- **Talk to her**. Women are verbal creatures and love to hear phrases that let them know how turned on you are, how much you love her body and how good you want to make her feel.

- **There is always room for improvement** – your lovemaking skills should get better with time. Always seek to improve your lovemaking abilities. Do not think that you know it all.

Female Sexual Arousal

According to American sex researchers William Masters and Virginia Johnson, women go through four stages in sexual arousal; the Excitement (or Arousal) phase, Plateau phase, Orgasmic phase and Resolution phase. Medical science's view of feminine erotic physiology remains pretty much the same today as it was when Masters and Johnson carried out their research in the 1960s. Below is a breakdown of the four phases of the female sexual arousal along with some tips.

1. **Excitement (or Arousal) Phase.** – The first stage in which some erotic stimulus, like

passionate kissing and sensual touching, begins to prepare the body ready for sexual intercourse. This stage is accompanied by a rise in heart rate and blood pressure, erection of the nipples and increased lubrication inside the vagina. She may become flushed, especially on the chest and neck, due to the dilating blood vessels.

Tip: Be delicate with your touches and sucking of her nipples as they are extremely sensitive during this period

2. **Plateau Phase.** A stage in which the female body starts to prepare itself for imminent orgasm. The clitoris becomes sensitive, and the tissues of the outer part of the vagina begin to swell. This is a critical stage as a woman is aroused, continuous stimulation is required in order to build up enough sexual excitement for orgasm.

   Some women require the same type of stimulation but for a longer period, other will require a different form of stimulation method, and there are those who may require the same type of penetrative stimulation but with firmer and faster thrusts.

Tip: Respond to her in order to know what type of stimulation is required to enable her to attain an orgasm. The wrong move could result in a decrease in her level of arousal, thus not being able to climax.

3. **Orgasmic Phase.** This stage is the stage of the orgasmic climax. The orgasm is the intense and pleasurable release of sexual tension that has built up in the earlier stages. It is characterised by immense enjoyment, and by a series of involuntary contractions in the pelvic muscles, and muscular spasms in various parts of the body.

   Deep breathing, gasping, the roll of the eyes, and a flush across a woman's chest are also signs that she is experiencing an orgasm. Orgasms often come on suddenly and can last for up to twenty seconds.

Tip: Maintain pressure to prolong the orgasm. The average female orgasm lasts for 6-10 seconds according to sexologists, but some women can keep coming[148] for 30 minutes minutes!

4. **Resolution Phase.** In the final stage, blood pressure, swelling and heart rate falls as a woman's body slowly returns to its normal state. However, if sexual stimulation continues, the resolution phase may be very short, and she may proceed to further (multiple) orgasms.

Tip: Women often feel happy and relaxed at this stage due to the "feel-good" hormones like dopamine and oxytocin running through her body. Orgasms are a form of sexual healing with many health benefits. After climaxing a woman is at her most relaxed state, a warm and firm embrace will make her feel extra special.

---

[148] "Keep coming" refers to having an orgasm or orgasms.

Multiple Orgasms

Multiple orgasms are the holy grail of sex.

The female orgasm is much more complicated and emotional driven than the male orgasm. The female orgasm lasts longer, is more intense, and is more pleasurable than their male counterparts. One of the fascinating factors about the female orgasm is that women have the ability to have multiple orgasms unlike most men.[149]

Women are blessed by the fact that they are able to experience multiple orgasms whilst men generally can only experience one. Unlike men, women do not require a refractory period (or rest) to have an additional orgasm, so they are able to stay aroused for a longer period and have multiple orgasms consecutively with little effort.

In order to help your lady achieve multiple orgasms, you should be mentally and physically prepared to put in the work. Some women require more work than others. Even if your woman is adequately aroused, the onus is still on you as the man to help her get to the thralls of physical ecstasy. There is nothing like giving a woman a toe-curling climax; feeling her body shake with delight, listening to her moan with joy, and watching her eyes roll as if she is in a trance. It is truly a great pleasure! Unfortunately many women have never experienced the joys of orgasms, even after a number of years of marriage!

---

[149] There are two types of multiple orgasms, sequential orgasms, which are a series of orgasms that are two to ten minutes apart, and serial orgasms, which come one after the other in rapid succession.

Multiple orgasms are extremely difficult to achieve for many women which is why many people think it does not exist. The truth of the matter is that multiple orgasms do exist and regular women are capable of having multiple climaxes with the right partner, good technique and a relaxed state of mind. Below are some practical steps to help give your lady multiple orgasms:

Mental Preparation – Becoming a multi-orgasmic woman has lot to do with a woman's mind-set. Many women do not allow themselves to get fully aroused, which is a problem as arousal is what fuels multiple orgasms. In order to achieve full arousal a woman must be mentally prepared and physically ready to enjoy the great pleasures of multiple orgasms. When a woman feels relaxed, is at ease and is comfortable in her surroundings, these factors will help mentally prepare her to experience the joys of multiple orgasm.

Breathing – After your lady has experienced her first orgasm you should encourage her to focus on breathing deeply and steadily, to help her relax. When women get sexually excited they tend to hold their breath which makes it harder to achieve another orgasm. Deep and steadily breathing can also help increase the power and pleasure of an orgasm.

Sweet-talking – After the first orgasm keep her mind sexually engaged with sweet words in her ear. You will be able to maintain her physical desire if you describe and tell her how wonderful she feels, and how beautiful she looks as she climaxes. Be creative and inventive with your words. The sexier and more comfortable your woman feels, the more likely she will be at ease to come again.

Lubricants – After an orgasm some women experience discomfort around the vaginal area as it is extremely sensitive, and can become sore. Soreness of the vaginal area will diminish any pleasure and can make it difficult for her to achieve another orgasm. Lubricants can help relieve this pain and relax her mind as you start to play with her body again.

Kegel Exercises are an effective way to help a woman last longer in bed and experience multiple orgasms. Kegel exercises strengthen the vaginal muscles as well as making the body ready for more pleasure.

Foreplay – Female-focused foreplay is one of the best techniques to keep her sexually stimulated for another orgasm. You should take your time and make her feel that your ultimate goal is to please her. Many women get very turned on when they feel that a man is devoting himself to her pleasure. This will help her relax more and increase the chances of her climaxing again.

Slow Sex and Pussy Sucking – A combination of slow rhythmic penetration and oral stimulation is a very effective method in helping a woman achieve multiple orgasms. It will enable you to connect emotionally with her and achieve an authentic female sexual satisfaction that is truly orgasmic.

Switch Stimulation – If she has just experienced a clitoral orgasm, you should then proceed to stimulate her G-Spot or vagina as it will provide her with a different type of sensation and can help give her another orgasm in the same sexual session. If she has just climaxed through intercourse, you should switch to giving her oral sex or manual stimulation. The variety of play will subconsciously encourage her to orgasm again.

Take Her to the Brink – Taking a woman to the brink of orgasm without letting her climax is one of the best ways you can get her to experience a truly intense and pleasurable orgasm that she will not forget. You must be disciplined to do this properly, especially because your woman might become frustrated and restless. As she is just about to climax you should stop stimulating her. This will prevent her from climaxing. You should take her to the brink of climax about four times before you allow her to orgasm in full. Her built up sexual tension will result in a shuddering burst of pleasure and often will lead to her being able to orgasm again quickly thereafter.

Extended Sexual Orgasm – Stroke her labia for 5 minutes without touching her clitoris, and tell her to breathe deeply and do pelvis floor squeezes. When you feel two-second contractions as she is about to come, move your fingers to stroke the inside of her vagina until she climaxes. After she has climaxed, move your fingers between her vagina and clitoris, stroking the area very gently which will lead to another wave of orgasms. This technique can keep a woman coming for a long time.

APPENDIX: EROTOLOGICAL WORKS

Akande, Habeeb, [2015, British-Nigerian], *A Taste of Honey: Sexuality and Erotology in Islam.*

Akande, Habeeb, [2015, British-Nigerian], *Illuminating the Difference: Black, Brown, and White Women.*

Al-Aqfahsi, Shihab al-Din [d. 1406, Egypt], *The Raising of the Wings as Regards the Lawful Woman.*

Al-Baghdadi, Abu Abd al-Rahman, [14th century, Egypt], *The Book of Delicate Flowers Regarding the Kiss and the Embrace.*

don Fodio, Usman, [d. 1804 West Africa], *Reviving the Sunnah.*

Al-Fallati, Muhammad Ibn Muhammad Tuqur, [d. 1741, Sudan], *Assistance of the Brothers Regarding the Association with Women.*

Al-Ghazālī, Abū Hamid, [d. 1111, Persia] *The Revival of the Islamic Sciences.*

Al-Ghazlawi, Muhammad Ibn Umar, [17th century], *Jasmine of the Scented Garden in the Excursion of Desire.*

Al-Hawrani, Abd al-Rahim, [14th century, Syria], *Uncovering the Secrets of Swindlers and the Laws of Tricksters.*

Al-Himsi, al-Muzaffar Ibn Nasir Ibn Ali al-Qurayshi, [d. 1215, Syria], *Treatise on Coitus.*

Hunayn Ibn Ishaq, [809-73, Iraq], *Book on the Secrets of the Philosophy of Coitus.*

Ibn Adi Yahya, [d. 974], *Book on the Benefits and Disadvantages of Coitus and the Ways of Practising it.*

Ibn al-Qayyim al-Jawziyyah (d. 1406), *The Garden of Lovers and Excursion of the Longing.*

Ibn Bukhtishu, Jibrail Ibn Jurjius, [d. 827, Persia], *The Book on Coitus.*

Ibn Falita al-Yamani, Ahmad Ibn Muhammad Ibn Ali Abu al-Abbas, [d. 1331, Yemen], *An Intelligent Man's Guide to Intercourse with a Loved One.*

Ibn Ḥabīb, 'Abd al-Mālik, *Treatise on the Proper Behaviour of Women.*

Ibn Hajib al-Nu;man, Muhammad Ibn Abd al-Aziz, [d. 1031], *The Book of Dancing Girls.*

Al-Ḥasanī, Aḥmad ibn Ismā ʿ ī al- ʿ Alawī [d. 1817, Morroco], *The Soul's Excursion regarding what Benefits the Bride and Groom.*

Ibn Hisham, Ahmad Ibn Ahmad, [15th century. Andalusia], *The Beauties of Women.*

Ibn Ishaq, Al, [mid-14th century], *Book on The Science of Coitus.*

Ibn Kannanm Muhammad Ibn Isa al-Khaluti, [1663-1740, Syria], *Excursion of the Souls, the Book of Science and the Garden of the Bride in Matters of Lawful Sexual Intercourse.*

Qusta Ibn Luqa, [820-912, Syria], *The Book on Coitus and what Regimen is Required to Practise It.*

Qusta Ibn Luqa, [820-912, Syria], *The Book on Coitus.*

Ibn Mandawayh, Abu Ali [d. 1019, Persia], *Treatise on the Reasons for Coitus.*

Ibn Marzuq, Shams al-Din Abu Abdullah [d. 1080, Tunis], *Vigilance Regarding the Treatment of Coitus.*

Ibn Massa, Isa, [9th century, Persia], *Questions about Progeny, Offspring and Coitus.*

Ibn Maymun (Maimonides), [1135-1204, Andalus], *[Treatise] On Coitus.*

Ibn al-Qatta, [1041-1121, Sicily], *The Book on the Language of Lawful Intercourse.*

Ibn Rahmun, Sallama, [d. 1136, Egypt], *Treatise on the Fertility of Egyptian Women's Bodies upon Expiration of Youth.*

Ibn Raqiqa, Mahmud Ibn Umar al-Shaybani, [d. 1169-1238, Turkey], *The Revelation of Doubts about Aphrodisiacs.*

Ibn Sina, [d. 1037, Persia], *Urjuza on Coitus.*

Ibn Sina, [d. 1037, Persia], *The Secrets of Lawful Intercourse.*

Ibn Sulayman, Ahmad, *Garden Flowers in the Knowledge of the Situations in which People Engage in Coitus.*

Ibn al-Takriti, Yahya Ibn Jarir, [second half of 11th century, Iraq], *The Book on Coitus, the Benefits of Intercourse and Its Harmful Effects.*

Ibn Yaḥyā al-Maghribī, [12th century], *Conversation of the Friends on the Companionship with the Beloved.*

Al-Isra'ili, Samaw'al Ibn Yahya Abbas al-Maghribi, [d. 1180], *The Friends' Jaunt in Coitus Between Lovers.*

Al-Isra'ili, Samaw'al Ibn Yahya Abbas al-Maghribi, [d. 1180], *The Book on Coitus.*

Al-Istānbūlī, Mahmoud Mahdī, *The Gift of the Bride or the Happy Islamic Marriage.*

-

Al-Jahiz, Abu Uthman, [d. 781-868, Iraq], *The Pleasure of Girls and Boys Compared.*

Al-Jahiz, Abu Uthman, [d. 781-868, Iraq], *The Book of Marriage and Brides.*

Al-Jahiz, Abu Uthman, [d. 781-868, Iraq], *[Treatise] On Women.*

Al-Jahiz, Abu Uthman, [d. 781-868, Iraq], *[Treatise] On Chanteuses.*

Al-Jildak, Idmar Ibn Ali Izz al-Din, [d. 1342. Egypt], *The Diver's Pearls and the Specialist Treasure regarding the Science of Characteristics.*

Al-Katib, Abu al-Hasan Ali Ibn Nasr al-Sammani, [10th century Baghdad]. *The Encyclopaedia of Pleasure.*

Al-Katib, Abu al-Hasan Ali Ibn Nasr al-Sammani, [10th century Baghdad]. *Book on the Chemistry of Coitus.*

Khan, Muhammad al-Sadq Hassan [d. 1878], *The Intoxication of the Drunkyard on the Wine of the Commemoration of Youths.*

Al-Khatib, Abu Nasr, *Book on the News of Women.*

Al-Khuwarizmi, Abu Bakr, [d. 993, Persia], *The Book on Coitus.*

Al-Kindi, [d. 873, Iraq], *The Book on Coitus.*

Al-Maghribi, Ibrahim, [first half 17th century, Morocco], *Categories of Coitus.*

Al-Masihi, Izz al-Din, *Coitus and Preamble to the Categories of Coitus and Its Tools.*

Al-Mufaddal, Ibn Umar, *The Book of Nonsense and Slips of the Tongue.*

Al-Mughaltay, al-Hafiz, [13th century], Clarity *Regarding the Memory of Those Who Were Martyed Because of the Loved Ones.*

Al-Nafzawi, Muhammad Ibn Muhammad, [16th century Tunis], *The Perfumed Garden of Sensual Delight.*

Al-Nafzawi, Muhammad Ibn Muhammad, [16th century Tunis], *Illuminating the Performance regarding the Secrets of Intercourse.*

Al-Namali, Hassan Ibn Muhammad, [9th century, Iraq], *The Book of Burjan and Hubahib.*

Al-Namali, Hassan Ibn Muhammad, [9th century, Iraq], *Address of the Muleteer to the Greengrocer's Slave Girl.*

Al-Namali, Hassan Ibn Muhammad, [9th century, Iraq], *The Book of Prostitution.*

Al-Namali, Hassan Ibn Muhammad, [9th century, Iraq], *The Book of Lesbianism.*

Al-Nawaj, Shams al-Din Muhammad Ibn Hasan [1386-1455, Egypt], *The Gazelles Pasture Regarding the Descriptions of the Beautiful among Boys.*

Al-Nihilli, *The Book on Coitus.*

Al-Qustantini, Mahmud Ibn Muhammad, [d. 1568, Tunis], *The Book of Medicines for Coitus.*

Al-Razi, Muhammad Ibn Zakariyya, [865-925, Persia], *The Book on Coitus, Its Benefits, Harmful Effects and Treatments.*

Al-Razi, Muhammad Ibn Zakariyya, [865-925, Persia], *Treatise on Whether Engaging in Coitus with Low Frequency Increases Lifespan.*

Al-Razi, Muhammad Ibn Zakariyya, [865-925, Persia], *Treatise on Passive Sodomy.*

Al-Sa'ati, Muhammad Raji al-Halabi, *The Sipping of Saliva and the Fruit of Lovers.*

Al-Saymari, Muhammad Ibn Ishaq Abu al-Anbas, [827-888, Iraq], *The Book on Lesbians and Homosexual Prostitutes.*

Al-Saymari, Muhammad Ibn Ishaq Abu al-Anbas, [827-888, Iraq], *The Book of Masturbation.*

Al-Saymari, Muhammad Ibn Ishaq Abu al-Anbas, [827-888, Iraq], *The Lover and the Loved One.*

Al-Saymari, Muhammad Ibn Ishaq Abu al-Anbas, [827-888, Iraq], *The Book of Rare Anecdotes on Eunuchs.*

Al-Saymari, Muhammad Ibn Ishaq Abu al-Anbas, [827-888, Iraq], *The Book of Rare Anecdotes on Pimps.*

Al-Saymari, Muhammad Ibn Ishaq Abu al-Anbas, [827-888, Iraq], *The Superiority of the Rectum Over the Mouth.*

Al-Shadhil, Abd al-Qadir Ibn Ahmad Ibn Muhammad al-Maliki, [d. 1529, Tunis], *Delighting the Ears by the Benefits of Hearing the Formula "In the Name of God" during Coitus.*

Al-Shafi'i, Ala al-Din, *[Treatise] On Lawful Intercourse.*

Al-Shayzari al-Tabari, Abd al-Rahman Ibn Nasr, [d. 1193, Egypt], *Elucidation of the Secrets of Lawful Intercourse.*

Al-Suyuti, Jalal al-Din, [d. 1505], *The Sash in the Benefits of Lawful Intercourse.*

Al-Suyuti, Jalal al-Din, [d. 1505], *The Sipping of the Pure Water of Lawful Charm.*

Al-Suyuti, Jalal al-Din, [d. 1505], *The Blooming of the Jungle in the Rareties of Fucking.*

Al-Suyuti, Jalal al-Din, [d. 1505], *Jungle in the Knowledge of Fucking.*

Al-Suyuti, Jalal al-Din, [d. 1505], *[Treatise] On Coitus and Its Tools.*

Al-Suyuti, Jalal al-Din, [d. 1505], *Halves of the Lemon Regarding the Intricacies of Coquetry.*

Al-Suyuti, Jalal al-Din, [d. 1505], *Excursion Regarding the Preferences of White, Black and Brown People.*

Al-Suyuti, Jalal al-Din, [d. 1505], *Height of Charity in the Creation of Human Beings.*

Al-Suyuti, Jalal al-Din, [d. 1505], *The Rules of Conduct for Lawful Intercourse and the Breaking of the Two Passions.*

Al-Suyuti, Jalal al-Din, [d. 1505], *Jaunt of the Table Companions in the Notification of Women.*

Al-Suyuti, Jalal al-Din, [d. 1505], *The Certainty of the Attachment Between the Lover and the One He Loves.*

Al-Suyuti, Jalal al-Din, [d. 1505], *The Foundation in He Who Is in Charge of the Cunt.*

Al-Suyuti, Jalal al-Din, [d. 1505], *Declaration regarding the Names for Lawful Intercourse.*

Al-Suyuti, Jalal al-Din, [d. 1505], *Precious Stones in the Description of the Fat Woman.*

Al-Suyuti, Jalal al-Din, [d. 1505], *Morning Ablutions in the Language of Lawful Intercourse.*

Al-Suyuti, Jalal al-Din, [d. 1505], *The Elegant Woman as regards Provisions for the Entry of the Glans Penis.*

Al-Suyuti, Jalal al-Din, [d. 1505], *The Elegant Man regarding News of Slave Girls.*

Al-Suyuti, Jalal al-Din, [d. 1505], *Excursion of the Boon Champion.*

Al-Suyuti, Jalal al-Din, [d. 1505], *Excursion of the Spouse and the Guide to His Wife Regarding the Virtues of Lawful Intercourse.*

Al-Suyuti, Jalal al-Din, [d. 1505], *The Mouths of Wittiness and the Foot Soles of the Morning in the Seasons of Lawful Intercourse.*

Al-Suyuti, Jalal al-Din, [d. 1505], *Cut Ginger in Coitus with Face Veiled Women.*

Al-Suyuti, Jalal al-Din, [d. 1505], *Elucidation of the Secrets of Lawful Intercourse.*

Al-Suyuti, Jalal al-Din, [d. 1505]. *The Hidden Treasure and the Loaded Star.*

Al-Tabari, Ali Abu al-Hasan Ibn Rabban, [9th century, Persia], *The Book of Elucidation Regarding the Fat and the Skinny, Stimulation of Coitus and Its Thwarting.*

Al-Tadaghi, Abu Salih Ibn Salih, *Gift of the Peasant regarding the Science of Lawful Intercourse.*

Al-Tahiri, Ibn al-Shah [9th century], *The Book of News on Catamites.*

Al-Tahiri, Ibn al-Shah [9th century], *The Book of News on Women.*

Al-Tahiri, Ibn al-Shah [9th century], *The Book of Prostitution and Its Pleasures.*

Al-Tahiri, Ibn al-Shah [9th century], *The Book of Masturbation.*

Al-Tamakruti, Muhammad Abdullah Ibn Muhammad Ibn Mas'ud al-Dar' i al-Tafjaruti, [10th – 11th centuries], *The Ripe Gardens in the Rules for Marrying off a Woman and Etiquette for Congregation.*

Tayfur, Ahmad Ibn Abu Tahir, [d. 893, Iraq], *Information about Women.*

Al-Tifashi, Shihab al-Din Ahmad Ibn Yusuf, [d. 1253, Tunis], *Delights of Hearts in Things that Cannot Be Found in Any Book.*

Al-Tifashi, Shihab al-Din Ahmad Ibn Yusuf (or author was Ibn Kemal Pesha), [d. 1253, Tunis], *Returning the Old Man His Youthful Sexual Potency.*

Al-Tifashi, Shihab al-Din Ahmad Ibn Yusuf, [d. 1253, Tunis], *Treatise on What Men and Women Need During Coitus and Its Harms and Benefits.*

Al-Tijani, Muhammad Ibn Ahmad, [11th to early 14th centuries, Tunis], *The Bride's Gift and the Delight of the Souls.*

Al-Tusi, Nasir al-Din, *The Book of Choice Sexual Stimulants and the Sultan's Mixtures.*

Al-Zahiri, Ali Ibn Muhammad, [d. 963, Iraq], *News about Boys.*

Al-Zahiri, Ali Ibn Muhammad, [d. 963, Iraq], *Prostitution and Its Pleasures.*

Al-Zahiri, Ali Ibn Muhammad, [d. 963, Iraq], *News about Women.*

Zarruq, Ahmad, [1442-1493, Morocco], *Lawful Intercourse.*

BIBLIOGRAPHY

Arabic Sources

Al-Jāḥiẓ, Abū 'Uthmān 'Amr, *Rasā'il al-Jāḥiẓ vol. 1.* Beirut: Dar al-Kutub al-'Ilmiyyah, 2000.

Al-Ṣuyūṭī, Jalal al-Din (Edited by Jūrj Kadr), *Fann al-Nikah fi al-Qur'an al-Karim wa al-Hadith al-Sharif wa al-Athar wa funun al-Zina wa al-Gunij wa mula'aba wa al-Juma'*, Vol 1, Beirut: Atlas Publishing, 2011.

Al-Ṣuyūṭī, Jalal al-Din (Edited by Jūrj Kadr), *Fann al-Nikaah fii turaath shaykh al-Islam Jalaal al-Diin al-Suyuti, Vol 2 – Akhbar al-Khulafa' wa Ahl al-'Ilm wa Al-Mustatrif min akhbar al-Jawari wa Jamilat al-Arab wa Maqamat al-Nisa' wa manakih al-Hayawanat,* Beirut: Atlas Publishing, 2011.

Ibn Hisham, Abū Ja'far Aḥmad ibn Aḥmad, *Mahasin al-Nisa'*, Cairo: Al-Tawfikia Bookshop, [no year of publication].

Ibn Majah, Abu Abdullah Muhammad, *Sunan Ibn Majah,* Riyadh: Dar al-Salam. 1999.

Ibn Yaḥyā, Abū Naṣr al-Samawal al-Maghribī, *Nuzhat al-aṣḥāb fi mu`āsharat al-aḥbāb,* Dar Al-Kotob Al-Ilmiyah: Beirut, 2008.

Ibn Yūsuf Tīfāshī, Aḥmad, *Rujū' al-shaykh ilá ṣibāh fī al-quwwah 'alá al-bāh,* Damscus: Dar al-Kitab al-'Arabi, 2011.

English Sources

Al-Jahiz, (trans. Jim Colville), *Sobriety and Mirth: A Selection of the Shorter Writings of al-Jāḥiẓ*. London: Keegan Paul, 2002.

Al-Nafzawi, Muhammad ibn Muhammad, (translated by Jim Colville), *The Perfumed Garden of Sensual Delight*, Keegan Paul: London, 1999.

Alaba, Olugboyega, *Understanding Sexuality in the Yoruba Culture*, Africa Regional Sexuality Resource Centre, 2004.

Akande, Habeeb, *A Taste of Honey: Sexuality and Erotology in Islam*, London: Rabaah Publishers, 2015.

Akande, Habeeb, *Illuminating the Difference: Black, Brown, and White Women*, London: Rabaah Publishers, 2015.

Ben-Zeév, Aaron, "Why Make-Up Sex And Breakup Sex Are So Good", *Psychology Today,* February 2013. https://www.psychologytoday.com/blog/in-the-name-love/201302/why-make-sex-and-breakup-sex-are-so-good (accessed March 24, 2015).

Bouhdiba, Abdelwahab (translated by Alan Sheridan), *Sexuality in Islam*, London: Saqi Books, 2004.

Comfort, Alex, "More Joy of Sex vol. 2," in *The Complete Joy of Sex,* London: Chancellor Press, 1987.

Comfort, Alex, "The Joy of Sex vol. 1," in *The Complete Joy of Sex,* London: Chancellor Press, 1987.

Daedone, Nicole, *Slow Sex: The Art and Craft of the Female Orgasm,* Grand Central Publishing, 2012.

Deida, David, *The Way of the Superior Man: A Spiritual Guide to Mastering the Challenges of Women, Work, and Sexual Desire*, Colorado: Sounds True, 2004.

Elam, Paul, On Studs and Sluts, *A Voice for Men,* 2012 http://www.avoiceformen.com/misandry/on-studs-and-sluts/ (accessed January 12, 2015).

Edewor, P.A., "The Influence of Religion on Contraception and Fertility" in Dopamu, P.A. (ed) *Science and Religion in the Service of Humanity,* Ilorin: (LSI) & (NASTRENS). 2006.

El-Feki, Shereen, et al, *The Institute of Sexology,* London: The Wellcome Trust, 2014.

Fadipe, N. A., *The Sociology of the Yoruba,* Ibadan: Ibadan University Press, 1970.

Familus, O. O., African Culture and the Status of Women: The Yoruba Example, in *The Journal of Pan African Studies*, vol. 5, no. 1, 2012.

Forberg, Friedrich Karl, *Manual of Classical Erotology,* Honolulu: University Press of the Pacific, 2002.

Foxcroft, Louise, *Sexuality: All That Matters,* London: Hodder and Stoughton, 2014.

Franke, Patrick, "Before scientia sexualis in Islamic cultures between erotology, medicine and pornography" in *Social Identities: Journal for the Study of Race, Nation and Cultrure*, Volume 18, Issue 2, 2012.

Gibson, Tyrese and Rev Run, *Manology: Secrets of Your Mans Mind Revealed*, London: Touchstone, 2014.

Greene, Robert, *The Art of Seduction*, London: Profile Books, 2003.

Harvey, Steve, *Act Like a Lady, Think Like a Man*, New York: Amistad, 2012.

Ibn Falita, Ahmad ibn Muhammad (Translated by Adnan Jarkas and Salah Addin Khawwam), *An Intelligent Man's Guide to the Art of Coition*, Edited by Salah Addin Khawwamm, Toronto: Aleppo, 1977.

Ibn Nasir al-Khatib, Abul Hasan Ali, (Translated by Adnan Jarkas and Salah Addin Khawwam), *Encyclopedia of Pleasure*, Edited by Salah Addin Khawwam, Toronto: Aleppo, 1977.

Johnson Hodari, Askhari, and McCalla Sobers, Yvonne, *Lifelines: The Black Book of Proverbs*, New York: Broadway Books, 2009.

Khalil, Mohammad, "An Unknown Aspect in the Life of Al-Jahiz," http://www.qsm.ac.il/ArbLanguage/docs/majalla/1/2-eng-khalil.pdf (accessed March 21, 2015)

Nasheed, Tariq, *The Mack Within: The Holy Book of Game*, London: Penguin, 2005.

Nasheed, Tariq, The Art of Mackin', [not stated]: G. D. Publishing, 2009.

Newman, David, *The Sultan's Sex Positions: Arab Aphrodisiacs in the Middle Ages*, London: Saqi Books, 2014.

Rosenau, Douglas, *A Celebration of Sex: A Guide to Enjoying God's Gift of Sexual Intimacy*, Tennessee: Thomas Nelson Inc., 2002.

Rudov, Marc, *The Man's No-Nonsense Guide to Women: How to Succeed in Romance on Planet Earth,* California, MHR Enterprises, 2004

Al-Suyuti, (translated by English Bohemian), *The Book of Exposition*, London: Darf Publishers, 1987.

Vatsyayana (translated by Richard Burton), *The Kama Sutra*, Croydon: Penguin Books, 1994.

Watkins, Boyce, "How Sleeping With The Wrong Woman Might Turn Your Into A "Rapist"," *BrothersOnSports,* December 2013. http://www.brothersonsports.com/dr-boyce-how-sleeping-with-the-wrong-woman-might-turn-you-into-a-rapist/ (accessed March 25, 2015).

ABOUT THE AUTHOR

Habeeb Akande is a British-born writer, historian and erotologist of Yoruba descent. He is an alumnus of al-Azhar University in Cairo, Egypt and Kingston University in the UK. He is also the author of the books; *Illuminating the Darkness: Blacks and North Africans in Islam. A Taste of Honey: Sexuality and Erotology in Islam,* and *Illuminating the Difference: Black, Brown, and White Women.*